Soups & Appetizers

Publisher & Creative Director: Nick Wells
Senior Editor: Sarah Goulding
Designer: Mike Spender
With thanks to: Theresa Bebbington and Gina Steer

The reader should note that Asian ingredients feature in several of the recipes provided in this book.
These are worth taking the time to source from Asian food shops.

A copy of the CIP data for this book is available from the British Library.

ISBN 13: 978-0-7607-8682-6
ISBN 10: 0-7607-8682-8

Printed and bound in China

1 3 5 7 9 10 8 6 4 2

Soups & Appetizers

Quick and Easy, Proven Recipes

General Editor: Gina Steer

BARNES & NOBLE
NEW YORK

Contents

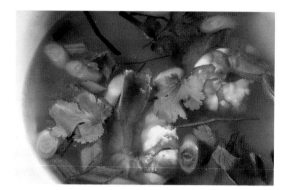

Appetizers: Fish & Shellfish — **98**

Appetizers: Poultry

Appetizers: Meat

Appetizers: Vegetables & Salads 240

Hygiene in the Kitchen

It is well worth remembering that many foods can carry some form of bacteria. In most cases the worst it will lead to is food poisoning or gastroenteritis, although for certain groups it can be more serious. The risk can be reduced or eliminated by good food hygiene and proper cooking.

Do not buy or use food that is past its expiration date. When buying fresh food, always use your eyes and nose. If the food looks tired, limp, or is a bad color, or if it has a rank, acrid, or simply bad smell, do not buy or eat it under any circumstances.

Regularly clean, defrost, and clear out the refrigerator or freezer. It is worth checking the packaging to see exactly how long each product is safe to freeze.

Wash and change dishcloths and kitchen towels regularly. Ideally use disposable cloths, which should be replaced on a daily basis. More durable cloths should be left to soak in

bleach, then washed in the washing machine on a hot setting.

Always keep your hands, cooking utensils, and food preparation surfaces clean, and never allow pets to climb onto any work surfaces.

Buying

Avoid bulk buying where possible, especially fresh produce such as meat, poultry, fish, fruit, and vegetables, unless buying them for the freezer. Fresh foods lose their nutritional value rapidly, so buying a little at a time minimizes the loss of nutrients. It also eliminates a packed refrigerator, which reduces the effectiveness of the refrigeration process.

When buying frozen foods ensure that they are not covered in ice on the outside. Place it in the freezer as soon as possible after purchase.

Preparation

Make sure that all work surfaces and utensils are clean and dry. Always use separate cutting boards for raw and cooked meats, fish, and vegetables. Wash all fruit and vegetables regardless of whether they will be eaten raw or lightly cooked. Do not reheat food more than once.

All poultry must be thoroughly thawed before cooking. Leave the food in the refrigerator until it is completely thawed. Once defrosted, the chicken should be cooked as soon as possible. The only time food can be refrozen is when the food has been thoroughly thawed then cooked. Once the food has cooled, it can be frozen again for one month.

All poultry and game (except for duck) must be cooked thoroughly. When cooked the juices will run clear. Other

meats, such as ground meat and pork, should always be cooked completely through. Fish should turn opaque, be firm in texture, and break easily into large flakes.

Storing, Refrigerating, and Freezing

Meat, poultry, fish, seafood, and dairy products should all be refrigerated. The temperature of the refrigerator should be set at 34–41°F, while the freezer temperature should not rise above -0.4°F. When refrigerating cooked food, allow it to cool down quickly and completely before refrigerating it. Hot food will raise the temperature of the refrigerator and possibly affect or spoil other food stored in it.

Food within the refrigerator and freezer should always be kept covered. Raw and cooked food should be stored in separate parts of the refrigerator. Cooked food should be kept on the top shelves of the refrigerator, while raw meat, poultry, and fish should always be placed on bottom shelves to avoid juices dripping onto and contaminating other foods.

High-Risk Foods

Certain foods may carry risks to people who are considered vulnerable, such as the elderly, the ill, pregnant women, babies, and those suffering from a recurring illness. It is advisable to avoid those foods that belong to a higher-risk category.

There is a slight chance that some eggs carry the bacteria salmonella. Cook the eggs until both the yolk and the white are firm to eliminate this risk. Sauces including Hollandaise, mayonnaise, mousses, soufflés, and meringues all use raw or slightly cooked eggs, as do custard-based dishes, ice creams, and sorbets. These are all considered high-risk foods for the vulnerable groups mentioned above. Certain meats and poultry also carry the potential risk of salmonella, so they should be cooked thoroughly until the juices run clear and there is no pinkness left. Unpasteurized products, such as milk, cheese (especially soft cheese), pâté, and meat (both raw and cooked) all have the potential risk of listeria and should be avoided.

When buying seafood, buy it from a reputable source. Fish should have bright clear eyes, shiny skin, and bright pink or red gills. The fish should feel stiff to the touch, and have a slight smell of sea air and iodine. The flesh of fish steaks and fillets should be translucent, with no signs of discoloration. Avoid any mollusks that are open or do not close when tapped lightly. Univalves, such as periwinkles, should withdraw into their shells when lightly prodded. Squid and octopus should have firm flesh and a pleasant sea smell.

Care is required when freezing seafood. It is imperative to check whether the fish has been frozen before. If it has been, then it should not be frozen again under any circumstances.

Nutrition
The Role of Essential Nutrients

A healthy and well-balanced diet is the body's primary energy source. In children it constitutes the building blocks for future health as well as providing a lot of energy. In adults it encourages healing and regeneration within the body. A well-balanced diet will provide the body with all the essential nutrients it needs. This can be achieved by eating a variety of foods, demonstrated in the pyramid below:

Fats
milk, yogurt,
and cheese
Proteins
meat, fish, poultry, eggs,
nuts, and legumes

Fruit and Vegetables

Starchy Carbohydrates
cereals, potatoes, bread, rice, and pasta

Fats

Fats fall into two categories: saturated and unsaturated fats. It is important that a healthy balance is achieved within the diet. Fats are an essential part of the diet, providing a source of energy, essential fatty acids, and fat-soluble vitamins. The right balance of fats should boost the body's immunity to infection and keep muscles, nerves, and arteries in good condition. Saturated fats are of animal origin and are hard when stored at room temperature. They can be found in dairy produce, meat, eggs, margarines, and hard white cooking fat (lard), as well as in manufactured products such as pies, cookies, and cakes. A high intake of saturated fat over many years has been proven to increase heart disease and high blood cholesterol levels and often leads to weight gain. The aim of a healthy diet is to keep the fat content low in the foods that we eat. Lowering the amount of saturated fat that we consume is important, but this does not mean that it is good to consume a lot of other types of fat.

There are two kinds of unsaturated fats: polyunsaturated fats and monounsaturated fats. Polyunsaturated fats include the following oils: safflower oil, soybean oil, corn oil, and sesame oil. Within the polyunsaturated group are Omega oils. The Omega-3 oils are of significant interest because they have been found to be particularly beneficial to coronary health and can encourage brain growth and development. Omega-3 oils are derived from oily fish, such as salmon, mackerel, herring, pilchards, and sardines. It is recommended that we should eat these types of fish at least once a week. However, for those who do not eat fish or who are vegetarians, liver oil supplements are available in most supermarkets and health stores. It is suggested that these supplements should be taken on a daily basis. The most popular oils that are high in monounsaturates are olive oil, sunflower oil, and peanut oil. The Mediterranean diet, which is based on a diet high in monounsaturated fats, is recommended for heart health. Also, monounsaturated fats are known to help reduce the levels of LDL (the bad) cholestrol.

Proteins

Composed of amino acids (proteins' building blocks), proteins perform a wide variety of essential functions for the body, including supplying energy and building and repairing tissues. Good sources of proteins are eggs, milk, yogurt, cheese, meat, fish, poultry, eggs, nuts, and legumes. (See the second level of the pyramid.) Some of these foods, however, contain saturated fats. To strike a nutritional balance eat generous amounts of vegetable protein foods, such as soy products, beans, lentils, peas, and nuts.

Fruit and Vegetables

Not only are fruit and vegetables the most visually appealing foods, but they are extremely good for us, providing essential vitamins and minerals that are vital for growth, repair, and protection in the human body. Fruit and vegetables are low in

calories and are responsible for regulating the body's metabolic processes and controlling the composition of its fluids and cells.

Minerals

CALCIUM This is important for healthy bones and teeth, nerve transmission, muscle contraction, blood clotting, and hormone function. Calcium promotes a healthy heart, improves skin, relieves aching muscles and bones, maintains the correct acid-alkaline balance, and reduces menstrual cramps. Good sources are dairy products, small bones of small fish, nuts, legumes, fortified flours, breads, and green leafy vegetables.

CHROMIUM Part of the glucose tolerance factor, chromium balances blood sugar levels, helps to normalize hunger and reduce cravings, improves lifespan, helps protect DNA, and is essential for heart function. Good sources are brewer's yeast, whole-wheat bread, rye bread, oysters, potatoes, green peppers, butter, and parsnips.

IODINE This is important for the manufacture of thyroid hormones and for normal development. Good sources of iodine are seafood, seaweed, milk, and dairy products.

IRON As a component of hemoglobin, iron carries oxygen around the body. It is vital for normal growth and development. Good sources are liver, corned beef, red meat, fortified breakfast cereals, legumes, green leafy vegetables, egg yolk, and cocoa and cocoa products.

MAGNESIUM It is important for the efficient functioning of metabolic enzymes and development of the skeleton. Magnesium promotes healthy muscles by helping them to relax and is therefore good for PMS. It is also important for heart muscles and the nervous system. Good sources are nuts, green vegetables, meat, cereals, milk, and yogurt.

PHOSPHORUS This forms and maintains bones and teeth, builds muscle tissue, helps maintain pH of the body, and aids energy production and metabolism. Phosphorus is in most foods.

POTASSIUM It enables nutrients to move into cells, while waste products move out; promotes healthy nerves and muscles; maintains fluid balance in the body; helps the secretion of insulin for blood sugar control to produce constant energy; relaxes muscles; maintains heart functioning; and stimulates gut movement to encourage proper elimination. Good sources are fruit, vegetables, milk, and bread.

SELENIUM The antioxidant properties of selenium help to protect against free radicals and carcinogens. Selenium reduces inflammation, stimulates the immune system to fight infections, promotes a healthy heart, and helps vitamin E's action. It is also required for the male reproductive system and is needed for metabolism. Good sources are tuna, liver, kidney, meat, eggs, cereals, nuts, and dairy products.

SODIUM It is important in helping to control body fluid and balance and preventing dehydration. Sodium is involved in muscle and nerve function and helps move nutrients into cells. All foods are good sources; however, processed, pickled, and salted foods are richest in sodium.

ZINC This is important for metabolism and the healing of wounds. It also aids ability to cope with stress, promotes a healthy nervous system and brain, especially in the growing fetus, aids bones and teeth formation, and is essential for constant energy. Good sources are liver, meat, legumes, whole-grain cereals, nuts, and oysters.

Vitamins

VITAMIN A This is important for cell growth and developmemt and for the formation of visual pigments in the eye. Vitamin A comes in two forms: retinol and beta-carotenes. Retinol is found in liver, meat, and meat products, whole milk and its products. Beta-carotene is a powerul antioxidant and is found in red and yellow fruit and vegetables, such as carrots and mangoes.

VITAMIN B_1 Important in releasing energy from carbohydrate-containing foods, good sources of vitamin B_1 are yeast and yeast products, bread, fortified breakfast cereals, and potatoes.

VITAMIN B_2 It is important for metabolism of proteins, fats, and carbohydrates to produce energy. Good sources are meat, yeast extracts, and milk and its products.

VITAMIN B_3 Required for metabolism of food into energy production, good sources of vitamin B_3 are milk and milk products, fortified breakfast cereals, legumes, poultry, and eggs.

VITAMIN B_5 It is important for metabolism of food and energy production. All foods are good sources, but especially fortified breakfast cereals, whole-grain bread, and dairy products.

VITAMIN B_6 Important for metabolism of protein and fat, vitamin B_6 may also be involved with the regulation of sex hormones. Good sources are liver, fish, pork, soy beans, and peanuts.

VITAMIN B₁₂ Important for the production of red blood cells and DNA. It is vital for growth and the nervous system. Good sources are meat, fish, eggs, poultry, and milk.

BIOTIN Important for the metabolism of fatty acids, good sources of biotin are liver, kidney, eggs, and nuts. Micro-organisms also manufacture this vitamin in the gut.

VITAMIN C It is important for healing wounds and the formation of collagen, which keeps skin and bones strong and is an important antioxidant. Good sources are fruits, berries (strawberries, raspberries, and blackberries), and vegetables.

VITAMIN D This is important for the absorption and handling of calcium to help build bone strength. Good sources are oily fish, eggs, whole milk and milk products, margarine, and, of course, sufficient exposure to sunlight, which allows vitamin D to be made in the skin.

VITAMIN E Important as an antioxidant vitamin, helping to protect cell membranes from damage, good sources of vitamin E are vegetable oils, margarines, nuts, and green vegetables.

FOLIC ACID It is critical during pregnancy for the development of the brain and nerves. It is always essential for brain and nerve function and is needed for utilizing protein and red blood cell formation. Good sources are whole-grain cereals, fortified breakfast cereals, green leafy vegetables, oranges, and liver.

VITAMIN K Important for controlling blood clotting, good sources of vitamin K are cauliflower, Brussels sprouts, lettuce, cabbage, beans, broccoli, peas, asparagus, potatoes, corn oil, tomatoes, and milk.

Carbohydrates

Carbohydrates are an energy source and come in two forms: starch and sugar carbohydrates. Starch carbohydrates are also known as complex carbohydrates, and they include all cereals, potatoes, breads, rice, and pasta. (See the fourth level of the pyramid.) Eating whole-grain varieties of these foods also provides fiber. Diets high in fiber are believed to be beneficial in helping to prevent bowel cancer and can help keep cholesterol down. High-fiber diets are also good for those concerned about weight gain. Fiber is bulky so it fills the stomach, therefore reducing hunger pangs. Sugar carbohydrates, which are also known as fast-release carbohydrates (because of the quick fix of energy they give to the body), include sugar and sugar-sweetened products, such as jams and syrups. Milk provides lactose, which is a milk sugar, and fruit provides fructose, which is a fruit sugar.

Soups

Tomato & Basil Soup

SERVES 4

5–6 medium tomatoes,
cut in half
2 garlic cloves
1 tsp olive oil
1 tbsp balsamic vinegar

1 tbsp dark brown sugar
1 tbsp tomato puree
1¼ cups vegetable stock
6 tbsp plain yogurt
2 tbsp freshly chopped basil

salt and freshly ground
black pepper
small basil leaves,
to garnish

Preheat the oven to 400°F. Evenly spread the tomatoes and unpeeled garlic in a single layer in a large roasting pan. Mix the oil and vinegar together. Drizzle over the tomatoes and sprinkle with the dark brown sugar. Roast the tomatoes in the preheated oven for 20 minutes, until tender and lightly charred in places.

Remove from the oven and let cool slightly. When cool enough to handle, squeeze the softened flesh of the garlic from the papery skin. Place with the charred tomatoes in a sieve over a saucepan.

Press the garlic and tomato through the sieve with the back of a wooden spoon. When all the flesh has been sieved, add the tomato puree and vegetable stock to the pan. Heat gently, stirring occasionally.

In a small bowl, beat the yogurt and basil together and season to taste with salt and pepper. Stir the basil yogurt into the soup. Garnish with basil leaves and serve immediately.

 Try this: FOR AN ALTERNATIVE: 40   FOR A LIGHT BITE: 182

Carrot & Ginger Soup

SERVES 4

4 slices of bread,
   crusts removed
2 tbsp olive or sunflower oil
   plus 2 tsp olive oil
1 onion, peeled
   and chopped
1 garlic clove, peeled
   and crushed

½ tsp ground ginger
6 carrots, peeled
   and chopped
4¼ cups vegetable stock
1-inch piece of fresh ginger,
   peeled and finely grated
salt and freshly ground
   black pepper

1 tbsp lemon juice

To garnish:
chives
lemon zest

Preheat the oven to 350°F. Roughly chop the bread, then gently toss it in 2 tablespoons of the olive oil.

Spread the bread cubes over a lightly oiled baking sheet and bake for 20 minutes, turning half way through. Remove from the oven and reserve.

Heat the remaining olive oil in a large saucepan. Gently cook the onion and garlic for 3–4 minutes. Stir in the ground ginger and cook for 1 minute to release the flavor. Add the chopped carrots, then stir in the stock and the fresh ginger. Simmer gently for 15 minutes.

Remove from the heat and let cool a little. Blend until smooth, then season to taste with salt and pepper. Stir in the lemon juice. Garnish with the chives and lemon zest and serve immediately.

Try this: FOR AN ALTERNATIVE: 28   FOR A LIGHT BITE: 230

Cream of Pumpkin Soup

SERVES 4

2 lb pumpkin flesh (after
    peeling and discarding
    the seeds)
4 tbsp olive oil
1 large onion, peeled
1 leek, trimmed

1 carrot, peeled
2 celery sticks
4 garlic cloves, peeled
    and crushed
7 cups water
salt and freshly ground

black pepper
¼ tsp freshly
    grated nutmeg
⅔ cup light cream
¼ tsp cayenne pepper
warm herb bread, to serve

Cut the skinned and deseeded pumpkin flesh into 1 inch cubes. Heat the olive oil in a large saucepan and cook the pumpkin for 2–3 minutes, coating it completely with oil. Chop the onion and leek finely and cut the carrot and celery into small cubes.

Add the vegetables to the saucepan with the garlic and cook, stirring for 5 minutes, or until they have begun to soften. Cover the vegetables with the water and bring to a boil. Season with plenty of salt and pepper and the nutmeg, cover, and simmer for 15–20 minutes, or until all of the vegetables are tender.

When the vegetables are tender, remove from the heat, cool slightly, then pour into a food processor or blender. Liquidize to form a smooth puree, then pass through a sieve into a clean saucepan.

Adjust the seasoning to taste and add all but 2 tablespoons of the cream and enough water to obtain the correct consistency. Bring the soup to boiling point, add the cayenne pepper, and serve immediately, swirled with the rest of the cream, with the warm herb bread.

Try this: FOR AN ALTERNATIVE: 26 FOR A LIGHT BITE: 104

Potato, Leek, & Rosemary Soup

SERVES 4

4 tbsp butter
1 lb leeks, trimmed and
 finely sliced
4–5 potatoes (about 1½ lb),
 peeled and roughly
 chopped

3¾ cups vegetable stock
4 sprigs of fresh rosemary
2 cups whole milk
2 tbsp freshly
 chopped parsley
2 tbsp crème fraîche or

sour cream
salt and freshly ground
 black pepper
whole-wheat rolls,
 to serve

Melt the butter in a large saucepan, add the leeks, and cook gently for 5 minutes, stirring frequently. Remove 1 tablespoon of the cooked leeks and reserve for garnishing.

Add the potatoes, vegetable stock, rosemary sprigs, and milk. Bring to a boil, then reduce the heat, cover, and simmer gently for 20–25 minutes, or until the vegetables are tender.

Cool for 10 minutes. Discard the rosemary, then pour into a food processor or blender and blend well to form a smooth-textured soup.

Return the soup to the cleaned saucepan and stir in the chopped parsley and crème fraîche. Season to taste with salt and pepper. If the soup is too thick, stir in a little more milk or water. Reheat gently without boiling, then ladle into warm soup bowls. Garnish the soup with the reserved leeks and serve immediately with whole-wheat rolls.

Try this: FOR AN ALTERNATIVE: 34 FOR A LIGHT BITE: 144

Cream of Spinach Soup

SERVES 6-8

1 large onion, peeled
   and chopped
5 large plump garlic cloves,
   peeled and chopped
2 medium potatoes, peeled
   and chopped
3 cups cold water

1 tsp salt
1 lb spinach, washed and
   large stems removed
4 tbsp butter
3 tbsp flour
3 cups milk
½ tsp freshly grated nutmeg

freshly ground black pepper
6–8 tbsp crème fraîche or
   sour cream
warm foccacia bread,
   to serve

Place the onion, garlic, and potatoes in a large saucepan and cover with the cold water. Add half the salt and bring to a boil. Cover and simmer for 15–20 minutes, or until the potatoes are tender. Remove from the heat and add the spinach. Cover and set aside for 10 minutes.

Make a white sauce in another saucepan. Slowly melt the butter, add the flour, and cook over a low heat for about 2 minutes. Remove the saucepan from the heat and add the milk, a little at a time, stirring continuously. Return to the heat and cook, stirring continuously, for 5–8 minutes, or until the sauce is smooth and slightly thickened. Add the freshly grated nutmeg, or to taste.

Blend the cooled potato and spinach mixture in a food processor or blender to a smooth puree, then return to the saucepan and gradually stir in the white sauce. Season to taste with salt and pepper and gently reheat, taking care not to let the soup boil. Ladle into soup bowls and top with spoonfuls of crème fraîche or sour cream. Serve immediately with warm foccacia bread.

Try this: FOR AN ALTERNATIVE: 78 FOR A LIGHT BITE: 130

Curried Parsnip Soup

SERVES 4

1 tsp cumin seeds
2 tsp coriander seeds
1 tsp oil
1 onion, peeled
   and chopped
1 garlic clove, peeled
   and crushed

½ tsp turmeric
¼ tsp chile powder
1 cinnamon stick
1 lb parsnips, peeled
   and chopped
4¼ cups vegetable stock
salt and freshly ground

black pepper
2–3 tbsp plain yogurt,
   to serve
fresh coriander leaves,
   to garnish

In a small frying pan, dry-fry the cumin and coriander seeds over a moderately high heat for 1–2 minutes. Shake the pan during cooking until the seeds are lightly toasted. Reserve until cooled. Grind the toasted seeds in a mortar and pestle.

Heat the oil in a saucepan. Cook the onion until softened and starting to turn golden. Add the garlic, turmeric, chile powder, and cinnamon stick to the pan. Continue to cook for a further minute.

Add the parsnips and stir well. Pour in the stock and bring to a boil. Cover and simmer for 15 minutes, or until the parsnips are cooked.

Allow the soup to cool. Once cooled, remove the cinnamon stick and discard. Blend the soup in a food processor until very smooth.

Transfer to a saucepan and reheat gently. Season to taste with salt and pepper. Garnish with fresh coriander and serve immediately with the yogurt.

Try this: FOR AN ALTERNATIVE: 96   FOR A LIGHT BITE: 244

Bacon & Split Pea Soup

SERVES 4

¼ cup dried split peas
2 tbsp butter
1 garlic clove, peeled and
finely chopped
1 medium onion, peeled
and thinly sliced
1 cup long-grain rice

2 tbsp tomato paste
4½ cups vegetable or
chicken stock
2 carrots, peeled and
finely diced
4 oz bacon, finely chopped
salt and freshly ground

black pepper
2 tbsp freshly
chopped parsley
4 tbsp light cream
warm garlic bread, to serve

Immerse the dried split peas in plenty of cold water, cover loosely, and let soak for a minimum of 12 hours, preferably overnight.

Melt the butter in a heavy-based saucepan, add the garlic and onion, and cook for 2–3 minutes, without coloring. Add the rice, drained split peas, and tomato paste, and cook for 2–3 minutes, stirring constantly to prevent sticking. Add the stock, bring to a boil, then reduce the heat and simmer for 20–25 minutes, or until the rice and peas are tender. Remove from the heat and let cool.

Blend about three-quarters of the soup in a food processor or blender to form a smooth puree. Pour the puree into the remaining soup in the saucepan. Add the carrots to the saucepan and cook for a further 10–12 minutes, or until the carrots are tender.

Meanwhile, place the bacon in a nonstick skillet and cook over a gentle heat until the bacon is crisp. Remove and drain on a paper towel.

Season the soup with salt and pepper to taste, then stir in the parsley and cream. Reheat for 2–3 minutes, then ladle into soup bowls. Sprinkle with the bacon and serve immediately with warm garlic bread.

Try this: FOR AN ALTERNATIVE: 24 FOR A LIGHT BITE: 252

Potato & Fennel Soup

SERVES 4

2 tbsp butter
2 large onions, peeled
    and thinly sliced
2–3 garlic cloves, peeled
    and crushed
1 tsp salt
3 potatoes (about 1 lb),

peeled and diced
1 fennel bulb, trimmed and
    finely chopped
½ tsp caraway seeds
4¼ cups vegetable stock
freshly ground
    black pepper

2 tbsp freshly
    chopped parsley
4 tbsp crème fraîche or
    sour cream
roughly torn pieces of
    French bread, to serve

Melt the butter in a large, heavy-based saucepan. Add the onions, the garlic, and half the salt, and cook over a medium heat, stirring occasionally, for 7–10 minutes, or until the onions are soft and begin to turn brown.

Add the potatoes, fennel bulb, caraway seeds, and the remaining salt. Cook for about 5 minutes, then pour in the vegetable stock. Bring to a boil, partially cover, and simmer for 15–20 minutes, or until the potatoes are tender. Stir in the chopped parsley and adjust the seasoning to taste.

For a smooth-textured soup, allow to cool slightly, then pour into a food processor or blender and blend until smooth. Reheat the soup gently, then ladle into individual soup bowls. For a chunky soup, omit this blending stage and ladle straight from the saucepan into soup bowls.

Swirl a spoonful of crème fraîche or sour cream into each bowl and serve immediately with roughly-torn pieces of French bread.

Try this: FOR AN ALTERNATIVE: 24 FOR A LIGHT BITE: 258

Pumpkin & Smoked Haddock Soup

SERVES 4

2 tbsp olive oil
1 medium onion, peeled
 and chopped
2 garlic cloves, peeled
 and chopped
3 celery stalks, trimmed
 and chopped

1½ lb pumpkin, peeled,
 deseeded, and cut
 into chunks
3 medium potatoes
 (about 1 lb), peeled
 and cut into chunks
3 cups chicken stock, heated

½ cup dry sherry
7 oz smoked haddock fillet
⅔ cup milk
freshly ground black pepper
2 tbsp freshly
 chopped parsley
3 tbsp water

Heat the oil in a large, heavy-based saucepan and gently cook the onion, garlic, and celery for about 10 minutes. This will release the sweetness but not color the vegetables. Add the pumpkin and potatoes to the saucepan and stir to coat the vegetables with the oil.

Gradually pour in the stock and bring to a boil. Cover, then reduce the heat and simmer for 25 minutes, stirring occasionally. Stir in the dry sherry, then remove the saucepan from the heat and let cool for 5–10 minutes. Blend the mixture in a food processor or blender to form a chunky puree and return to the cleaned saucepan.

Meanwhile, place the fish in a shallow skillet. Pour in the milk with 3 tablespoons of water and bring to almost a boiling point. Reduce the heat, cover, and simmer for 6 minutes, or until the fish is cooked and flakes easily. Remove from the heat and, using a slotted spoon, remove the fish from the liquid. Reserve both the liquid and the fish.

Discard the skin and any bones from the fish and flake into pieces. Stir the fish liquid into the soup, together with the flaked fish. Season with freshly ground black pepper, stir in the parsley, and serve immediately.

Try this: FOR AN ALTERNATIVE: 54 FOR A LIGHT BITE: 322

Rutabaga, Turnip, Parsnip, & Potato Soup

SERVES 4

2 large onions, peeled
2 tbsp butter
2 medium carrots, peeled
and roughly chopped
1 cup rutabaga, peeled and
roughly chopped
1 medium turnip, peeled

and roughly chopped
1 medium parsnip, peeled
and roughly chopped
1 large potato, peeled
and roughly chopped
4¼ cups vegetable stock
½ tsp freshly grated nutmeg

salt and freshly ground
black pepper
4 tbsp vegetable oil,
for frying
½ cup heavy cream
warm crusty bread, to serve

Finely chop 1 onion. Melt the butter in a large saucepan and add the onion, carrots, rutabaga, turnip, parsnip, and potato. Cover and cook gently for about 10 minutes, without coloring. Stir occasionally during this time.

Add the stock and season to taste with the nutmeg, salt, and pepper. Cover and bring to a boil, then reduce the heat and simmer gently for 15–20 minutes, or until the vegetables are tender. Remove from the heat and let cool for 30 minutes.

Heat the oil in a large, heavy-based skillet. Add the remaining, finely chopped, onion and cook over a medium heat for about 2–3 minutes, stirring frequently, until golden brown. Remove the onions with a slotted spoon and drain well on a paper towel. As they cool, they will turn crispy.

Pour the cooled soup into a food processor or blender and process to form a smooth puree. Return to the cleaned pan, adjust the seasoning, then stir in the cream. Gently reheat and top with the crispy onions. Serve immediately with chunks of warm crusty bread.

Try this: FOR AN ALTERNATIVE: 30 FOR A LIGHT BITE: 254

Mushroom & Sherry Soup

SERVES 4

4 slices day-old white bread
zest of ½ lemon
1 tbsp lemon juice
salt and freshly ground
    black pepper
1½ cups assorted wild

mushrooms, lightly rinsed
1½ cups baby mushrooms,
    cleaned
2 tsp olive oil
1 garlic clove, peeled
    and crushed

6 green onions, trimmed
    and diagonally sliced
2½ cups chicken stock
4 tbsp dry sherry
1 tbsp freshly snipped
    chives, to garnish

Preheat the oven to 350˚F. Remove the crusts from the bread and cut the bread into small cubes. In a large bowl, toss the cubes of bread with the lemon zest and juice, 2 tablespoons of water, and plenty of freshly ground black pepper.

Spread the bread cubes onto a lightly oiled, large baking sheet and bake for 20 minutes, until golden and crisp. Reserve croutons until soup is ready.

If the wild mushrooms are small, leave some whole. Otherwise, thinly slice all the mushrooms and reserve. Heat the oil in a saucepan. Add the garlic and green onions and cook for 1–2 minutes. Add the mushrooms and cook for 3–4 minutes, until they start to soften. Add the chicken stock and stir to mix.

Bring to a boil, then reduce the heat to a gentle simmer. Cover and cook for 10 minutes. Stir in the sherry, and season to taste with a little salt and pepper. Pour into warmed bowls, sprinkle over the chives, and serve immediately with the lemon croutons.

Try this: FOR AN ALTERNATIVE: 46   FOR A LIGHT BITE: 318

Roasted Red Pepper, Tomato, & Red Onion Soup

SERVES 4

fine spray of oil
2 large red bell peppers,
    deseeded and
    roughly chopped
1 red onion, peeled and
    roughly chopped

3 medium tomatoes, halved
1 small crusty French stick
1 garlic clove, peeled
2½ cups vegetable stock
salt and freshly ground
    black pepper

1 tsp Worcestershire sauce
4 tbsp plain yogurt

Preheat the oven to 375°F. Spray a large roasting pan with the oil and place the bell peppers and onion in the base. Cook in the oven for 10 minutes. Add the tomatoes and cook for a further 20 minutes, or until the peppers are soft.

Cut the bread into ½-inch slices. Cut the garlic clove in half and rub the cut edge of the garlic over the bread. Place all the bread slices on a large baking sheet, and bake in the preheated oven for 10 minutes, turning halfway through, until golden and crisp.

Remove the vegetables from the oven and let cool slightly, then blend in a food processor until smooth. Strain the vegetable mixture through a large sieve into a saucepan to remove the seeds and skin. Add the stock, season to taste with salt and pepper, and stir to mix. Heat the soup gently until piping hot.

In a small bowl, beat together the Worcestershire sauce with the yogurt. Pour the soup into warmed bowls and swirl a spoonful of the yogurt mixture into each bowl. Serve immediately with the garlic toasts.

Try this: FOR AN ALTERNATIVE: 26 FOR A LIGHT BITE: 312

Chinese Chicken Soup

SERVES 4

8 oz cooked chicken
1 tsp oil
6 green onions, trimmed
    and diagonally sliced
1 red chile pepper, deseeded
    and finely chopped
1 garlic clove, peeled

    and crushed
1-inch piece fresh ginger,
    peeled and finely grated
4¼ cups chicken stock
5 oz medium egg noodles
1 carrot, peeled and cut
    into matchsticks

1 cup bean sprouts
2 tbsp soy sauce
1 tbsp fish sauce
fresh cilantro leaves,
    to garnish

Remove any skin from the chicken. Place on a cutting board and use two forks to tear the chicken into fine shreds.

Heat the oil in a large saucepan and fry the green onions and chile pepper for 1 minute. Add the garlic and ginger, and cook for another minute. Stir in the chicken stock and gradually bring the mixture to a boil.

Break up the noodles a little and add to the boiling stock with the carrot. Stir to mix, then reduce the heat to a simmer and cook for 3–4 minutes. Add the shredded chicken, bean sprouts, soy sauce, and fish sauce, and stir.

Cook for a further 2–3 minutes until piping hot. Ladle the soup into bowls and sprinkle with the cilantro leaves. Serve immediately.

Try this: FOR AN ALTERNATIVE: 52 FOR A LIGHT BITE: 192

Shrimp & Chile Soup

SERVES 4

2 green onions, trimmed
8 oz raw, large shrimp
3 cups fish stock
finely grated rind and juice
    of 1 lime

1 tbsp fish sauce
1 red chile pepper, deseeded
    and chopped
1 tbsp soy sauce
1 lemon grass stalk

2 tbsp rice vinegar
4 tbsp freshly
    chopped cilantro

To make green onion curls, finely shred the green onions lengthways. Place in a bowl of iced cold water and reserve.

Remove the heads and shells from the shrimp, leaving the tails intact. Split the shrimp almost in two to form a butterfly shape and individually remove the black thread that runs down the back of each one.

In a large pan, heat the stock with the lime rind and juice, fish sauce, chile pepper, and soy sauce. Bruise the lemon grass by crushing it along its length with a rolling pin, then add to the stock mixture.

When the stock mixture is boiling, add the shrimp and cook until they are pink. Remove the lemon grass and add the rice vinegar and cilantro.

Ladle into bowls and garnish with the green onion curls. Serve immediately.

Try this: FOR AN ALTERNATIVE: 34 FOR A LIGHT BITE: 286

Hot & Sour Mushroom Soup

SERVES 4

4 tbsp sunflower oil
3 garlic cloves, peeled and finely chopped
3 shallots, peeled and finely chopped
2 large red chile peppers, deseeded and finely chopped
1 tbsp soft brown sugar
large pinch of salt

4¼ cups vegetable stock
1¼ cups Thai fragrant rice
5 kaffir lime leaves, torn (optional)
2 tbsp soy sauce
grated rind and juice of 1 lemon
3¾ cups oyster mushrooms, cleaned and cut into pieces

2 tbsp freshly chopped coriander
To garnish:
2 green chile peppers, deseeded and finely chopped
3 green onions, trimmed and finely chopped

Heat the oil in a skillet, add the garlic and shallots, and cook until golden brown and starting to crisp. Remove from the pan and reserve. Add the red chile peppers to the pan and cook until they start to change color.

Place the garlic, shallots, and chile peppers in a food processor or blender and blend to a smooth puree with ⅔ cup of water. Pour the puree back into the pan, add the sugar with a large pinch of salt, then cook gently, stirring, until dark in color. Avoid burning the mixture.

Pour the stock into a large saucepan, add the garlic puree, rice, lime leaves (if using), soy sauce, and the lemon rind and juice. Bring to a boil, then reduce the heat, cover, and simmer gently for about 10 minutes.

Add the mushrooms and simmer for a further 10 minutes, or until the mushrooms and rice are tender. Remove the lime leaves, stir in the chopped coriander, and ladle into bowls. Place the chopped green chile peppers and green onions in small bowls and serve separately to sprinkle on top of the soup.

Try this: FOR AN ALTERNATIVE: 56   FOR A LIGHT BITE: 194

Clear Chicken & Mushroom Soup

SERVES 4

2 large chicken legs
  (about 1 lb)
1 tbsp peanut oil
1 tsp sesame oil
1 onion, peeled and
  thinly sliced
1-inch piece fresh ginger,
  peeled and finely chopped

4½ cups clear chicken stock
1 lemon grass stalk, bruised
¼ cup long-grain rice
1¼ cups mushrooms,
  cleaned and finely sliced
4 green onions, trimmed,
  cut into 2-inch pieces,
  and shredded

1 tbsp dark soy sauce
4 tbsp dry sherry
salt and freshly ground
  black pepper

Skin the chicken legs and remove any fat. Cut each in half to make two thigh and two drumstick portions and reserve. Heat the peanut and sesame oils in a large saucepan. Add the sliced onion and cook gently for 10 minutes, or until soft but not beginning to color.

Add the chopped ginger to the saucepan and cook for about 30 seconds, stirring all the time to prevent it from sticking, then pour in the stock. Add the chicken pieces and the lemon grass, cover, and simmer gently for 15 minutes. Stir in the rice and cook for a further 15 minutes, or until the chicken is cooked.

Remove the chicken from the saucepan and let it cool enough to handle. Finely shred the flesh, then return to the saucepan with the mushrooms, green onions, soy sauce, and sherry. Simmer for 5 minutes, or until the rice and mushrooms are tender. Remove the lemon grass.

Season the soup to taste with salt and pepper. Ladle into warmed serving bowls, making sure each has an equal amount of shredded chicken and vegetables, and serve immediately.

Try this: FOR AN ALTERNATIVE: 58 FOR A LIGHT BITE: 298

Creamy Chicken & Tofu Soup

SERVES 4-6

8 oz firm tofu, drained
3 tbsp peanut oil
1 garlic clove, peeled and crushed
1-inch piece fresh ginger, peeled and finely chopped
1-inch piece fresh galangal, peeled and finely sliced (if available)

1 lemon grass stalk, bruised
¼ tsp ground turmeric
2½ cups chicken stock
2½ cups coconut milk
2 cups cauliflower (about 8 oz), cut into tiny florets
1 medium carrot, peeled and cut into thin matchsticks

1 cup green beans, trimmed and cut in half
3 oz thin egg noodles
8 oz cooked chicken, shredded
salt and freshly ground black pepper

Cut the tofu into ½-inch cubes, then pat dry on a paper towel. Heat 1 tablespoon of the oil in a nonstick skillet. Fry the tofu in two batches for 3–4 minutes, or until golden brown. Remove, drain on a paper towel, and reserve.

Heat the remaining oil in a large saucepan. Add the garlic, ginger, galangal, and lemon grass, and cook for about 30 seconds. Stir in the turmeric, then pour in the stock and coconut milk, and bring to a boil. Reduce the heat to a gentle simmer, add the cauliflower and carrots, and simmer for 10 minutes. Add the green beans and simmer for a further 5 minutes.

Meanwhile, bring a large saucepan of lightly salted water to a boil. Add the noodles, turn off the heat, cover, and let cook; or cook according to the package instructions.

Remove the lemon grass from the soup. Drain the noodles and stir into the soup with the chicken and browned tofu. Season to taste with salt and pepper, then simmer gently for 2–3 minutes, or until heated through. Serve immediately in warmed soup bowls.

Try this: FOR AN ALTERNATIVE: 22   FOR A LIGHT BITE: 350

Wonton Noodle Soup

SERVES 4

4 shiitake mushrooms,
    cleaned
4 oz raw shrimp, peeled and
    finely chopped
4 oz ground pork
4 water chestnuts,
    finely chopped
4 green onions, trimmed
    and finely sliced
1 medium egg white
salt and freshly ground
    black pepper
1½ tsp cornstarch
1 package fresh
    wonton wrappers
4½ cups chicken stock
¾-inch piece fresh ginger,
    peeled and sliced
3 oz thin egg noodles
1½ cups pak choi, shredded

Place the mushrooms in a bowl, cover with warm water, and let soak for 1 hour. Drain, remove and discard the stalks, and finely chop the mushrooms. Return to the bowl with the shrimp, pork, water chestnuts, 2 of the green onions, and the egg white. Season to taste with salt and pepper. Mix well.

Mix the cornstarch with 1 tablespoon of cold water to make a paste. Place a wonton wrapper on a board and brush the edges with the paste. Drop a little less than 1 teaspoon of the pork mixture in the center, then fold in half to make a triangle, pressing the edges together. Bring the two outer corners together, fixing together with a little more paste. Continue until all the pork mixture is used up —you should have 16–20 wontons.

Pour the stock into a large, wide saucepan, add the ginger slices, and bring to a boil. Add the wontons and simmer for about 5 minutes. Add the noodles and cook for 1 minute. Stir in the pak choi and cook for a further 2 minutes, or until the noodles and pak choi are tender and the wontons have floated to the surface and are cooked through.

Ladle the soup into warmed bowls, discarding the ginger. Sprinkle with the remaining sliced green onion and serve immediately.

Try this: FOR AN ALTERNATIVE: 46   FOR A LIGHT BITE: 372

Thai Shellfish Soup

SERVES 4-6

12 oz raw shrimp
12 oz firm white fish, such as
    monkfish, cod, or haddock
6 oz small squid rings
1 tbsp lime juice
1 lb live mussels

1¾ cups coconut milk
1 tbsp peanut oil
2 tbsp Thai red curry paste
1 lemon grass stalk, bruised
3 kaffir lime leaves, finely
    shredded (optional)

2 tbsp Thai fish sauce
salt and freshly ground
    black pepper
fresh cilantro leaves,
    to garnish

Peel the shrimp. Using a sharp knife, remove the black vein along the back of the shrimp. Pat dry with a paper towel and reserve. Skin the fish, pat dry, and cut into 1-inch chunks. Place in a bowl with the shrimp and the squid rings. Sprinkle with the lime juice and reserve.

Scrub the mussels, removing their beards and any barnacles. Discard any mussels that are open, damaged, or that do not close when tapped. Place in a large saucepan and add ⅔ cup of coconut milk. Cover, bring to a boil, then simmer for 5 minutes, or until the mussels open, shaking the saucepan occasionally. Lift out the mussels, discarding any unopened ones, strain the liquid through a muslin-lined sieve, and reserve both the mussels and liquid.

Rinse and dry the saucepan. Heat the peanut oil, add the curry paste, and cook for 1 minute, stirring all the time. Add the lemon grass, lime leaves (if using), and fish sauce, and pour in both the strained and the remaining coconut milk. Bring the contents of the saucepan to a gentle simmer.

Add the fish mixture to the saucepan and simmer for 2–3 minutes, or until just cooked. Stir in the mussels, with or without their shells (depending on your preference). Season to taste with salt and pepper, then garnish with the cilantro leaves. Ladle into warmed bowls and serve immediately.

Try this: FOR AN ALTERNATIVE: 44 FOR A LIGHT BITE: 228

Thai Hot & Sour Shrimp Soup

SERVES 6

1½ lb raw, large shrimp
2 tbsp vegetable oil
3–4 stalks lemon grass, outer leaves discarded and coarsely chopped
1-inch piece fresh ginger, peeled and finely chopped
2–3 garlic cloves, peeled and crushed
small bunch fresh cilantro, leaves stripped and reserved, stems finely chopped
½ tsp freshly ground black pepper
7½ cups water
1–2 small red chile peppers, deseeded and thinly sliced
1–2 small green chile peppers, deseeded and thinly sliced
6 kaffir lime leaves, thinly shredded (optional)
4 green onions, trimmed and diagonally sliced
1–2 tbsp Thai fish sauce
1–2 tbsp freshly squeezed lime juice

Remove the heads from the shrimp by twisting them away from the body and reserve. Peel the shrimp, leaving the tails on, and reserve the shells with the heads. Using a sharp knife, remove the black vein from the back of the shrimp. Rinse and dry the shrimp and reserve. Rinse and dry the heads and shells.

Heat a wok, add the oil, and, when hot, add the shrimp heads and shells, the lemon grass, ginger, garlic, cilantro stems, and black pepper, and stir-fry for 2–3 minutes, or until the shrimp heads and shells turn pink and all the ingredients are colored. Carefully add the water to the wok and return to a boil, skimming off any scum that rises to the surface. Simmer over a medium heat for 10 minutes, or until slightly reduced. Strain through a sieve and return the clear shrimp stock to the wok.

Bring the stock back to a boil and add the reserved shrimp, chile peppers, lime leaves (if using), and green onions, and simmer for 3 minutes, or until the shrimp turn pink. Season with the fish sauce and lime juice. Spoon into heated soup bowls, dividing the shrimp evenly, and float a few cilantro leaves over the surface.

Try this: FOR AN ALTERNATIVE: 72   FOR A LIGHT BITE: 196

Coconut Chicken Soup

SERVES 4

2 lemon grass stalks
3 tbsp vegetable oil
3 medium onions, peeled
　and finely sliced
3 garlic cloves, peeled
　and crushed
2 tbsp fresh ginger,
　finely grated
2–3 kaffir lime leaves

(optional)
1½ tsp turmeric
1 red bell pepper, deseeded
　and diced
13½-oz can coconut milk
4½ cups vegetable or
　chicken stock
1½ cups easy-cook
　long-grain rice

10 oz cooked chicken meat
10-oz can corn kernels,
　drained
3 tbsp freshly
　chopped cilantro
1 tbsp Thai fish sauce
freshly chopped, pickled
　chile peppers, to serve

Discard the outer leaves of the lemon grass stalks, then place on a cutting board and, using a mallet or rolling pin, pound gently to bruise; reserve.

Heat the vegetable oil in a large saucepan and cook the onions over a medium heat for about 10–15 minutes, until soft and beginning to change color.

Lower the heat, stir in the garlic, ginger, lime leaves (if using), and turmeric, and cook for 1 minute. Add the red bell pepper, coconut milk, stock, lemon grass, and rice. Bring to a boil, cover, and simmer gently over a low heat for about 10 minutes.

Cut the chicken into bite-sized pieces, then stir into the soup with the corn kernels and the freshly chopped cilantro. Add a few dashes of the Thai fish sauce to taste, then reheat gently, stirring frequently. Serve immediately with a few chopped pickled chillies to sprinkle on top.

Try this: FOR AN ALTERNATIVE: 50 FOR A LIGHT BITE: 344

Wonton Soup

SERVES 4

For the chicken stock:
2 lb chicken or chicken
   pieces
1–2 onions, peeled
   and quartered
2 carrots, peeled
   and chopped
2 celery stalks, trimmed
   and chopped
1 leek, trimmed
   and chopped
2 garlic cloves,

unpeeled and lightly
   crushed
1 tbsp black peppercorns
2 bay leaves
small bunch parsley,
   stems only
2–3 slices fresh ginger,
   peeled (optional)
14 cups cold water

For the soup:
18 wontons
2–3 Chinese cabbage leaves,
   or a handful of spinach,
   shredded
1 small carrot, peeled and
   cut into matchsticks
2–4 green onions, trimmed
   and diagonally sliced
soy sauce, to taste
handful flat-leaf parsley,
   to garnish

Chop the chicken into six to eight pieces and put into a large stockpot or saucepan of water with the remaining stock ingredients. Place over a high heat and bring to a boil, skimming off any scum that rises to the surface. Reduce the heat and simmer for 2–3 hours, skimming occasionally. Strain the stock through a fine sieve or muslin-lined sieve into a large bowl. Let cool, then chill in the refrigerator for 5–6 hours, or overnight. When cold, skim off the fat and remove any small pieces of fat by dragging a piece of kitchen towel lightly across the surface.

Bring a medium saucepan of water to a boil. Add the wontons and return to a boil. Simmer for 2–3 minutes, or until the wontons are cooked, stirring frequently. Rinse under cold running water, drain, and reserve. Pour 1¼ cups of stock per person into a large wok. Bring to a boil over a high heat, skimming any foam that rises to the surface, and simmer for 5–7 minutes to reduce slightly. Add the wontons, Chinese cabbage leaves or spinach, carrots, and green onions. Season with a few drops of soy sauce and simmer for 2–3 minutes. Garnish with a few parsley leaves and serve immediately.

Try this: FOR AN ALTERNATIVE: 42 FOR A LIGHT BITE: 260

Corn & Crab Soup

SERVES 4

1 lb fresh ears of sweet corn
5½ cups chicken stock
2–3 green onions, trimmed
    and finely chopped
½-inch piece fresh ginger,
    peeled and finely chopped
1 tbsp dry sherry or
    Chinese rice wine

2–3 tsp soy sauce
1 tsp light brown sugar
salt and freshly ground
    black pepper
2 tsp cornstarch
8 oz white crabmeat,
    fresh or canned
1 medium egg white

1 tsp sesame oil
1–2 tbsp freshly
    chopped cilantro

Wash the ears of sweet corn and dry. Using a sharp knife, and holding the ears at an angle to the cutting board, cut down along the ears to remove the kernels, then scrape the ears to remove any excess milky residue. Put the kernels and the milky residue into a large wok.

Add the chicken stock to the wok and place over a high heat. Bring to a boil, stirring and pressing some of the kernels against the side of the wok to squeeze out the starch – this helps thicken the soup. Simmer for 15 minutes, stirring occasionally.

Add the green onions, ginger, sherry or Chinese rice wine, soy sauce, and brown sugar to the wok, and season to taste with salt and pepper. Simmer for a further 5 minutes, stirring occasionally. Blend the cornstarch with 1 tablespoon of cold water to form a smooth paste and whisk into the soup. Return to a boil, then simmer over medium heat until thickened.

Add the crabmeat, stirring until blended. Beat the egg white with the sesame oil and stir into the soup in a slow steady stream, stirring constantly. Stir in the chopped cilantro and serve immediately.

Try this: FOR AN ALTERNATIVE: 44   FOR A LIGHT BITE: 168

Hot & Sour Soup

SERVES 4-6

1 oz dried shiitake
  mushrooms
2 tbsp peanut oil
1 carrot, peeled and cut
  into matchsticks
1½ cups chestnut
  mushrooms, cleaned and
  thinly sliced
2 garlic cloves, peeled and
  finely chopped

½ tsp dried crushed
  chile flakes
4½ cups chicken stock
  (see page 60)
3 oz cooked boneless
  chicken or pork, shredded
4 oz fresh tofu, thinly sliced
  (optional)
2–3 green onions,
  trimmed and finely

  sliced diagonally
1–2 tsp sugar
3 tbsp cider vinegar
2 tbsp soy sauce
salt and freshly ground
  black pepper
1 tbsp cornstarch
1 large egg
2 tsp sesame oil
2 tbsp freshly chopped

Place the dried shiitake mushrooms in a small bowl and pour over enough almost boiling water to cover. Let soak for 20 minutes to soften, then gently lift out and squeeze out the liquid. (Lifting out the mushrooms leaves any sand and grit behind.) Discard the stems, thinly slice the caps, and reserve.

Heat a large wok and add the oil; when it is hot, add the carrot strips and stir-fry for 2–3 minutes, or until beginning to soften. Add the chestnut mushrooms and stir-fry for another 2–3 minutes, or until golden, then stir in the garlic and chile flakes. Add the chicken stock to the vegetables and bring to a boil, skimming any foam that rises to the surface. Add the shredded chicken or pork, tofu (if using), green onions, sugar, vinegar, soy sauce, and reserved shiitake mushrooms, and simmer for 5 minutes, stirring occasionally. Season to taste with salt and pepper.

Blend the cornstarch with 1 tablespoon of cold water to form a smooth paste and whisk into the soup. Return to a boil and simmer over a medium heat until thickened. Beat the egg with the sesame oil and slowly add to the soup in a slow, steady stream, stirring constantly. Stir in the chopped cilantro and serve the soup immediately.

Try this: FOR AN ALTERNATIVE: 48 FOR A LIGHT BITE: 268

Chinese Cabbage & Mushroom Soup

SERVES 4–6

1 lb Chinese cabbage leaves
1 oz dried shiitake
    mushrooms
1 tbsp vegetable oil
3 oz smoked bacon, diced
1-inch piece fresh ginger,
    peeled and finely chopped

2½ cups chestnut
    mushrooms,
    thinly sliced
4½ cups chicken stock
4–6 green onions, trimmed
    and cut into short lengths
2 tbsp dry sherry or Chinese

rice wine
salt and freshly ground
    black pepper
sesame oil for drizzling

Trim the stem ends of the Chinese cabbage leaves and cut in half lengthways. Remove the triangular core with a knife, then cut into 1-inch slices and reserve.

Place the dried shiitake mushrooms in a bowl and pour over enough almost boiling water to cover. Let stand for 20 minutes to soften, then gently lift out and squeeze out the liquid. Discard the stems, thinly slice the caps, and reserve. Strain the liquid through a muslin-lined sieve or a coffee filter paper and reserve.

Heat a wok over a medium-high heat and add the oil; when hot, add the bacon. Stir-fry for 3–4 minutes, or until crisp and golden, stirring frequently. Add the ginger and chestnut mushrooms and stir-fry for a further 2–3 minutes. Add the chicken stock and bring to a boil, skimming any fat and scum that rises to the surface. Add the green onions, sherry or rice wine, Chinese cabbage leaves, and sliced shiitake mushrooms. Season to taste with salt and pepper. Pour in the reserved soaking liquid and reduce the heat to the lowest possible setting.

Simmer gently, covered, until all the vegetables are tender; this will take about 10 minutes. Add a little water if the liquid has reduced too much. Spoon into soup bowls and drizzle with a little sesame oil. Serve immediately.

Try this: FOR AN ALTERNATIVE: 38 FOR A LIGHT BITE: 366

Vietnamese Beef & Rice Noodle Soup

SERVES 4-6

For the beef stock:
2 lb beef, still on the bones
1 large onion, peeled
and quartered
2 carrots, peeled and
cut into chunks
2 celery stalks, trimmed
and sliced
1 leek, washed and sliced
into chunks

2 garlic cloves,
unpeeled and
lightly crushed
3 whole star anise
1 tsp black peppercorns

For the soup:
6 oz dried rice stick noodles
4–6 green onions, trimmed
and diagonally sliced

1 red chile pepper, deseeded
and diagonally sliced
1 small bunch fresh cilantro
1 small bunch fresh mint
12 oz fillet steak,
thinly sliced
salt and freshly ground
black pepper

Place all the ingredients for the beef stock into a large stockpot or saucepan and cover with cold water. Bring to a boil and skim off any scum that rises to the surface. Reduce the heat and simmer gently, partially covered, for 2–3 hours, skimming occasionally.

Strain into a large bowl and let cool; then skim off the fat. Chill in the refrigerator and, when cold, remove any fat from the surface. Pour 7 cups of the stock into a large wok and reserve.

Cover the noodles with warm water and let stand for 3 minutes, or until just softened. Drain, then cut into 4-inch lengths. Arrange the green onions and chile pepper on a serving platter or large plate. Strip the leaves from the cilantro and mint and arrange them in piles on the plate.

Bring the stock in the wok to a boil over a high heat. Add the noodles and simmer for about 2 minutes, or until tender. Add the beef strips and simmer for about 1 minute. Season to taste with salt and pepper. Ladle the soup with the noodles and beef strips into individual soup bowls and serve immediately with the plate of condiments.

Try this: FOR AN ALTERNATIVE: 48 FOR A LIGHT BITE: 308

Laksa Malayan Rice Noodle Soup

SERVES 4-6

2½ lb chicken
1 tsp black peppercorns
1 tbsp vegetable oil
1 large onion, peeled and
    thinly sliced
2 garlic cloves, peeled and
    finely chopped
1-inch piece fresh ginger,
    peeled and thinly sliced
1 tsp ground coriander

2 red chile peppers,
    deseeded and
    diagonally sliced
1–2 tsp hot curry paste
1¾ cups coconut milk
1 lb large, raw shrimp,
    peeled and de-veined
½ small head of Chinese
    cabbage, thinly shredded
1 tsp sugar

2 green onions, trimmed
    and thinly sliced
1 cup bean sprouts
9 oz rice noodles or rice
    sticks, soaked as per
    package instructions
fresh mint leaves, to garnish

Put the chicken in a large saucepan with the peppercorns and cover with cold water. Bring to a boil, skimming off any scum that rises to the surface. Simmer, partially covered, for about 1 hour. Remove the chicken and cool. Skim any fat from the stock and strain through a muslin-lined sieve and reserve. Remove the meat from the carcass, shred, and reserve.

Heat a large wok and add the oil; when hot, add the onions and stir-fry for 2 minutes, or until they begin to color. Stir in the garlic, ginger, coriander, chile peppers, and curry paste, and stir-fry for a further 2 minutes.

Carefully pour in the reserved stock (you need at least 4½ cups) and simmer gently, partially covered, for 10 minutes, or until slightly reduced. Add the coconut milk, shrimp, Chinese cabbage, sugar, green onions, and bean sprouts, and simmer for 3 minutes, stirring occasionally. Add the reserved shredded chicken and cook for a further 2 minutes.

Drain the noodles and divide between four to six soup bowls. Ladle the hot stock and vegetables over the noodles, making sure each serving has some shrimp and chicken. Garnish each bowl with fresh mint leaves and serve immediately.

Beef Noodle Soup

SERVES 4

2 lb boneless round
   or braising steak
1 cinnamon stick
2 star anise
2 tbsp light soy sauce
6 dried red chile peppers

or 3 fresh red chile
   peppers, chopped in half
2 dried citrus peels, soaked
   and diced (optional)
4½ cups beef or
   chicken stock

12 oz egg noodles
2 green onions, trimmed
   and chopped, to garnish
chunks of warm crusty
   bread, to serve (optional)

Trim the meat of any fat and sinew, then cut into thin strips. Place the meat, cinnamon, star anise, soy sauce, red chile peppers, chopped citrus peels (if using), and stock into the wok. Bring to a boil, then reduce the heat to a simmer. Skim any fat or scum that floats to the surface. Cover the wok and simmer for about 1½ hours, or until the meat is tender.

Meanwhile, bring a saucepan of lightly salted water to a boil, then add the noodles and cook in the boiling water for 3–4 minutes, until tender; or cook according to the package directions. Drain well and reserve.

When the meat is tender, add the noodles to the wok and simmer for a further 1–2 minutes, until the noodles are heated through thoroughly. Ladle the soup into warm, shallow soup bowls or dishes and scatter with chopped green onions. Serve, if you want, with chunks of warm crusty bread.

Sour & Spicy Shrimp Soup

SERVES 4

2 oz rice noodles	2½ cups chicken stock	12 raw, large shrimp,
1 oz dried shiitake	1-inch piece fresh ginger,	peeled, with the tail
mushrooms	peeled and grated	shell left on
4 green onions, trimmed	2 lemon grass stalks, outer	2 tbsp Thai fish sauce
2 small green chile peppers	leaves discarded and	2 tbsp lime juice
3 tbsp freshly chopped	finely chopped	salt and freshly ground
cilantro	4 kaffir lime leaves (optional)	black pepper

Place the noodles in cold water and let soak while preparing the soup. Place the dried mushrooms in a small bowl, cover with almost boiling water, and let soak for 20–30 minutes. Drain, strain, and reserve the soaking liquid; discard any woody stems from the mushrooms.

Finely shred the green onions and place into a small bowl. Cover with ice cold water and refrigerate until required and the green onions have curled.

Place the green chile peppers with 2 tablespoons of the chopped cilantro in a pestle and mortar and pound to a paste. Reserve.

Pour the stock into a saucepan and bring gently to a boil. Stir in the ginger, lemon grass, and lime leaves (if using) with the reserved mushrooms and their liquor. Return to a boil.

Drain the noodles and add to the soup with the shrimp, Thai fish sauce, and lime juice, then stir in the chile and cilantro paste. Bring to a boil, then simmer for 3 minutes. Stir in the remaining chopped cilantro and season to taste with salt and pepper. Ladle into warmed bowls, sprinkle with the green onion curls, and serve immediately.

Try this: FOR AN ALTERNATIVE: 44   FOR A LIGHT BITE: 248

Creamy Caribbean Chicken & Coconut Soup

SERVES 4

6–8 green onions
2 garlic cloves
1 red chile pepper
6 oz cooked chicken,
   shredded or diced
2 tbsp vegetable oil
1 tsp ground turmeric

1¼ cups coconut milk
3¾ cups chicken stock
2 oz small pasta shapes,
   or spaghetti broken
   into small pieces
½ lemon, sliced
salt and freshly ground

black pepper
1–2 tbsp freshly
   chopped cilantro
sprigs of fresh cilantro,
   to garnish

Trim the green onions and thinly slice them, then peel the garlic and finely chop it. Cut the top off the chile pepper, slit down the side, and remove the seeds and membrane; then finely chop the pepper and reserve.

Remove and discard any skin or bones from the cooked chicken and shred it, using two forks, and reserve.

Heat a large wok and add the oil; when hot, add the green onions, garlic, and chile pepper. Stir-fry for 2 minutes, or until the onion has softened. Stir in the turmeric and cook for 1 minute.

Blend the coconut milk with the chicken stock until smooth, then pour into the wok. Add the pasta or spaghetti with the lemon slices and bring to a boil. Simmer, half-covered, for 10–12 minutes, or until the pasta is tender; stir occasionally.

Remove the lemon slices from the wok and add the chicken. Season to taste with salt and pepper and simmer for 2–3 minutes, or until the chicken is heated through thoroughly.

Stir in the chopped cilantro and ladle into heated bowls. Garnish with sprigs of fresh cilantro and serve immediately.

Try this: FOR AN ALTERNATIVE: 36   FOR A LIGHT BITE: 242

Rice & Tomato Soup

SERVES 4

¾ cup easy-cook basmati rice
14-oz can chopped tomatoes
2 garlic cloves, peeled
    and crushed
grated rind of ½ lime
2 tbsp extra virgin olive oil
1 tsp sugar

salt and freshly
    ground pepper
1¼ cups vegetable stock
    or water

For the croutons:
2 tbsp prepared pesto sauce
2 tbsp olive oil
6 thin slices ciabatta bread,
    cut into ½-inch cubes

Preheat the oven to 425°F. Rinse and drain the basmati rice. Place the canned tomatoes with their juice in a large, heavy-based saucepan with the garlic, lime rind, oil, and sugar. Season to taste with salt and pepper. Bring to a boil, then reduce the heat, cover, and simmer for 10 minutes.

Add the boiling vegetable stock or water and the rice, then cook, uncovered, for a further 15–20 minutes, or until the rice is tender. If the soup is too thick, add a little more water. Reserve and keep warm if the croutons are not ready.

Meanwhile, to make the croutons, mix the pesto and olive oil in a large bowl. Add the bread cubes and toss until they are coated completely with the mixture. Spread on a baking sheet and bake in the preheated oven for 10–15 minutes, until golden and crisp, turning them over halfway through cooking. Serve the soup immediately, sprinkled with the warm croutons.

Try this: FOR AN ALTERNATIVE: 18   FOR A LIGHT BITE: 348

Bread & Tomato Soup

SERVES 4

2 lb ripe tomatoes
4 tbsp olive oil
1 onion, peeled and
   finely chopped
1 tbsp freshly chopped basil
3 garlic cloves, peeled

   and crushed
¼ tsp hot chile powder
salt and freshly ground
   black pepper
2½ cups chicken stock
6–7 slices stale white bread

⅛ cucumber, diced
4 whole basil leaves

Make a small cross in the base of each tomato, then place in a bowl and cover with boiling water. Let stand for 2 minutes, or until the skins have started to peel away; then drain, remove the skins and seeds, and chop into large pieces.

Heat 3 tablespoons of the olive oil in a saucepan and gently cook the onion until softened. Add the skinned tomatoes, chopped basil, garlic, and chile powder, and season to taste with salt and pepper. Pour in the stock, cover the saucepan, bring to a boil, and simmer gently for 15–20 minutes.

Remove the crusts from the bread and break into small pieces. Remove the tomato mixture from the heat and stir in the bread. Cover and let stand for 10 minutes, or until the bread has blended with the tomatoes. Season to taste. Serve warm or cold with a swirl of olive oil on the top and garnished with a spoonful of chopped cucumber and basil leaves.

Try this: FOR AN ALTERNATIVE: 40 FOR A LIGHT BITE: 134

Italian Bean Soup

SERVES 4

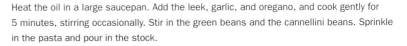

2 tsp olive oil
1 leek, washed and chopped
1 garlic clove, peeled
   and crushed
2 tsp dried oregano
1⅓ cups green beans,

trimmed and cut into bite-
   sized pieces
14½-oz can cannellini beans,
   drained and rinsed
3 oz small pasta shapes
4¼ cups vegetable stock

8 cherry tomatoes
salt and freshly ground
   black pepper
3 tbsp freshly shredded basil

Heat the oil in a large saucepan. Add the leek, garlic, and oregano, and cook gently for 5 minutes, stirring occasionally. Stir in the green beans and the cannellini beans. Sprinkle in the pasta and pour in the stock.

Bring the stock mixture to a boil, then reduce the heat to a simmer. Cook for 12–15 minutes, or until the vegetables are tender and the pasta is cooked but still firm. Stir occasionally.

In a heavy-based skillet, dry-fry the tomatoes over a high heat until they soften and the skins begin to blacken. Gently crush the tomatoes in the pan with the back of a spoon and add them to the soup.

Season to taste with salt and pepper. Stir in the shredded basil and serve immediately.

Try this: FOR AN ALTERNATIVE: 92 FOR A LIGHT BITE: 138

White Bean Soup with Parmesan Croutons

SERVES 4

3 thick slices of white bread,
    cut into ½-inch cubes
3 tbsp peanut oil
¼ cup Parmesan cheese,
    finely grated
1 tbsp light olive oil
1 large onion, peeled and
    finely chopped
2 oz unsmoked, thickly

    sliced bacon, diced
1 tbsp fresh thyme leaves
2 x 14-oz can cannellini
    beans, drained
3¾ cups chicken stock
salt and freshly ground
    black pepper
1 tbsp prepared pesto sauce
2 oz pepperoni, diced

1 tbsp fresh lemon juice
1 tbsp fresh basil,
    roughly shredded

Preheat the oven to 400°F. Place the cubes of bread in a bowl and pour over the peanut oil. Stir to coat the bread, then sprinkle over the Parmesan cheese. Place on a lightly oiled baking sheet and bake in the preheated oven for 10 minutes, or until crisp and golden.

Heat the olive oil in a large saucepan and cook the onion for 4–5 minutes, until softened. Add the bacon and thyme and cook for a further 3 minutes. Stir in the beans, stock, and black pepper, and simmer gently for 5 minutes.

Place half the bean mixture and liquid into a food processor and blend until smooth. Place the puree in a saucepan. Stir in the pesto sauce, pepperoni, and lemon juice, and season to taste with salt and pepper.

Return the soup to the heat and cook for a further 2–3 minutes, or until piping hot. Place some of the pureed beans in each serving bowl and add a ladleful of soup. Garnish with shredded basil and serve immediately with the croutons scattered over the top.

Rice Soup with Potato Sticks

SERVES 4

¾ cup (1½ sticks) butter
1 tsp olive oil
1 large onion, peeled and
    finely chopped
4 slices Parma ham or
    prosciutto, chopped
½ cup arborio or risotto rice

4½ cups chicken stock
2⅓ cups frozen peas
salt and freshly ground
    black pepper
1 medium egg
1 cup all-purpose flour
¾ cup mashed potato

1 tbsp milk
1 tbsp poppy seeds
2 tbsp Parmesan cheese,
    finely grated
1 tbsp freshly
    chopped parsley

Preheat the oven to 375°F. Heat 2 tablespoons of the butter and the olive oil in a saucepan. Cook the onion for 4–5 minutes until softened, then add the ham and cook for about 1 minute. Stir in the rice, the stock, and the peas. Season to taste with salt and pepper, and simmer for 10–15 minutes, or until the rice is tender.

Beat the egg and ½ cup of the butter together until smooth, then beat in the flour, a pinch of salt, and the mashed potato. Work the ingredients together to form a soft, pliable dough, adding a little more flour if necessary.

Roll the dough out on a lightly floured surface into a rectangle, ½-inch thick, and cut into 12 long, thin sticks. Brush with milk and sprinkle on the poppy seeds. Place the sticks on a lightly oiled baking sheet and bake in the preheated oven for 15 minutes, or until golden.

When the rice is cooked, stir the remaining butter and Parmesan cheese into the soup and sprinkle the chopped parsley over the top. Serve immediately with the warm potato sticks.

Try this: FOR AN ALTERNATIVE: 78 FOR A LIGHT BITE: 300

Rich Tomato Soup with Roasted Red Peppers

SERVES 4

2 tsp light olive oil
1½ lb red bell peppers,
   halved
1 lb ripe plum tomatoes,
   halved

2 onions, unpeeled
   and quartered
4 garlic cloves, unpeeled
2½ cups chicken stock
salt and freshly ground

black pepper
4 tbsp sour cream
1 tbsp freshly shredded basil

Preheat the oven to 400˚F. Lightly oil a roasting pan with 1 teaspoon of the olive oil. Place the peppers and tomatoes cut-side down in the roasting pan with the onion quarters and the garlic cloves. Spoon over the remaining oil.

Bake in the preheated oven for 30 minutes, or until the skins on the peppers start to blacken and blister. Allow the vegetables to cool for about 10 minutes, then remove the skins, stalks, and seeds from the peppers. Peel away the skins from the tomatoes and onions, and squeeze out the garlic.

Place the cooked vegetables into a blender or food processor and blend until smooth. Add the stock and blend again to form a smooth puree. Pour the pureed soup through a sieve if a smooth soup is preferred, then pour into a saucepan. Bring to a boil, simmer gently for 2–3 minutes, and season to taste with salt and pepper. Serve hot with a swirl of sour cream and a sprinkling of shredded basil on the top.

Try this: FOR AN ALTERNATIVE: 34 FOR A LIGHT BITE: 330

Arugula & Potato Soup with Garlic Croutons

SERVES 4

14–18 baby new potatoes
   (about 1½ lb)
4½ cups chicken or vegetable
   stock
2 cups arugula
4 thick slices white bread
4 tbsp unsalted butter

1 tsp peanut oil
2–4 garlic cloves, peeled
   and chopped
1 stale ciabatta roll, with
   the crusts removed
4 tbsp olive oil
salt and freshly ground

black pepper
¼ cup Parmesan cheese,
   finely grated

Place the potatoes in a large saucepan, cover with the stock, and simmer gently for 10 minutes. Add the arugula and simmer for a further 5–10 minutes, or until the potatoes are soft and the arugula has wilted.

Meanwhile, make the croutons. Cut the thick, white sliced bread into small cubes and reserve. Heat the butter and peanut oil in a small skillet and cook the garlic for 1 minute, stirring well. Remove the garlic. Add the bread cubes to the butter and oil mixture in the skillet and fry, stirring continuously, until they are golden brown. Drain the croutons on a paper towel and reserve.

Cut the ciabatta roll into small cubes and stir into the soup. Cover the saucepan and let stand for 10 minutes, or until the bread has absorbed a lot of the liquid.

Stir in the olive oil, season to taste with salt and pepper, and serve at once with a few of the garlic croutons scattered over the top, and a little grated Parmesan cheese.

Try this: FOR AN ALTERNATIVE: 32   FOR A LIGHT BITE: 162

Classic Minestrone

SERVES 6-8

2 tbsp butter
3 tbsp olive oil
3 slices bacon
1 large onion, peeled
1 garlic clove, peeled
1 celery stick, trimmed
2 carrots, peeled

14-oz can chopped tomatoes
4½ cups chicken stock
2½ cups green cabbage,
   finely shredded
½ cup green beans,
   trimmed and halved
3 tbsp frozen small peas

2 oz spaghetti, broken
   into short pieces
salt and freshly ground
   black pepper
Parmesan cheese shavings,
   to garnish
crusty bread, to serve

Heat the butter and olive oil together in a large saucepan. Chop the bacon and add to the saucepan. Cook for 3–4 minutes, then remove with a slatted spoon and reserve.

Finely chop the onion, garlic, celery, and carrots, and add to the saucepan, one ingredient at a time, stirring well after each addition. Cover and cook gently for 8–10 minutes, until the vegetables are softened.

Add the chopped tomatoes, with their juice, and the stock, bring to a boil; then cover the saucepan with a lid, reduce the heat, and simmer gently for about 20 minutes.

Stir in the cabbage, beans, peas, and spaghetti pieces. Cover and simmer for a further 20 minutes, or until all the ingredients are tender. Season to taste with salt and pepper.

Return the cooked bacon to the saucepan and bring the soup to a boil. Serve the soup immediately with Parmesan cheese shavings sprinkled on the top and plenty of crusty bread to accompany it.

Try this: FOR AN ALTERNATIVE: 80 FOR A LIGHT BITE: 108

Lettuce Soup

SERVES 4

2 heads of iceberg
   lettuce, cored
1 tbsp olive oil
4 tbsp butter
7 green onions, trimmed
   and chopped

1 tbsp freshly
   chopped parsley
1 tbsp all-purpose flour
2½ cups chicken stock
salt and freshly ground
   black pepper

⅔ cup light cream
¼ tsp cayenne pepper,
   to taste
thick slices of stale
   ciabatta bread
sprig of parsley, to garnish

Bring a large saucepan of water to a boil and blanch the lettuce leaves for 3 minutes. Drain and dry thoroughly on a paper towel, then shred with a sharp knife.

Heat the oil and butter in a clean saucepan and add the lettuce, green onions, and parsley, and cook together for 3–4 minutes, or until soft.

Stir in the flour and cook for 1 minute, then gradually pour in the stock, stirring throughout. Bring to a boil and season to taste with salt and pepper. Reduce the heat, cover, and simmer gently for 10–15 minutes, or until soft.

Allow the soup to cool slightly, then either sieve or puree it in a blender. Alternatively, leave the soup chunky. Stir in the cream, add more seasoning if you want, then add the cayenne pepper.

Arrange the slices of ciabatta bread in a large soup dish or in individual bowls and pour the soup over the bread. Garnish with sprigs of parsley and serve immediately.

Try this: FOR AN ALTERNATIVE: 20 FOR A LIGHT BITE: 328

Pasta & Bean Soup

SERVES 4-6

3 tbsp olive oil
2 celery sticks, trimmed and
    finely chopped
3½ oz prosciutto,
    cut into pieces
1 red chile pepper, deseeded
    and finely chopped
2 large potatoes, peeled and
    cut into 1-inch cubes

2 garlic cloves, peeled and
    finely chopped
3 ripe plum tomatoes,
    skinned and chopped
14-oz can cannellini beans,
    drained and rinsed
4¼ cups chicken or
    vegetable stock
13½ oz pasta shapes

large handful basil
    leaves, torn
salt and freshly ground
    black pepper
shredded basil leaves,
    to garnish
crusty bread, to serve

Heat the olive oil in a heavy-based pan, add the celery and prosciutto, and cook gently for 6–8 minutes, or until softened. Add the chopped chile pepper and potato cubes, and cook for a further 10 minutes.

Add the garlic to the chile and potato mixture and cook for 1 minute. Add the chopped tomatoes and simmer for 5 minutes. Stir in two-thirds of the beans, then pour in the chicken or vegetable stock and bring to a boil. Add the pasta shapes to the soup stock and return it to simmering point. Cook the pasta for about 10 minutes, or until firm.

Meanwhile, place the remaining beans in a food processor or blender and blend with enough of the soup stock to make a smooth, thinnish puree.

When the pasta is cooked, stir in the pureed beans with the torn basil. Season the soup to taste with salt and pepper. Ladle into serving bowls, garnish with shredded basil, and serve immediately with plenty of crusty bread.

Try this: FOR AN ALTERNATIVE: 84 FOR A LIGHT BITE: 124

Appetizers: Fish & Shellfish

Barbecued Fish Kebabs

SERVES 4

1 lb herring or mackerel
   fillets, cut into chunks
2 small red onions,
   peeled and quartered
16 cherry tomatoes

salt and freshly ground
   black pepper
For the sauce:
⅔ cup fish stock
5 tbsp ketchup

2 tbsp Worcestershire sauce
2 tbsp wine vinegar
2 tbsp brown sugar
2 drops Tabasco
2 tbsp tomato paste

Line a broiler rack with a single layer of foil and preheat the broiler to a high temperature, 2 minutes before use. If using wooden skewers, soak in cold water for 30 minutes to prevent them from catching fire during cooking.

Meanwhile, prepare the sauce. Add the fish stock, ketchup, Worcestershire sauce, vinegar, sugar, Tabasco, and tomato paste to a small saucepan. Stir well and simmer for 5 minutes.

When ready to cook the kebabs, drain the skewers (if necessary), then thread the fish chunks, quartered red onions, and cherry tomatoes alternately onto the skewers.

Season the kebabs to taste with salt and pepper and brush with the sauce. Broil under the preheated broiler for 8–10 minutes, basting with the sauce occasionally during cooking. Turn the kebabs often to ensure that they are cooked thoroughly and evenly on all sides. Serve immediately with couscous.

Try this: FOR AN ALTERNATIVE: 218   FOR KIDS: 144

Mixed Salad with Anchovy Dressing & Ciabatta Croutons

SERVES 4

1 small head endive
1 small head chicory
1 fennel bulb
14-oz can artichokes,
   drained and rinsed
½ cucumber
4 oz cherry tomatoes

3 oz black olives

For the anchovy dressing:
1¾ oz- can anchovy fillets
1 tsp Dijon mustard
1 small garlic clove, peeled
   and crushed

4 tbsp olive oil
1 tbsp lemon juice
freshly ground black pepper

For the ciabatta croutons:
2 thick slices ciabatta bread
2 tbsp olive oil

Divide the endive and chicory into leaves and reserve some of the larger ones. Arrange the smaller leaves in a wide salad bowl.

Cut the fennel bulb in half from the stalk to the root end, then cut across in fine slices. Quarter the artichokes, then quarter and slice the cucumber, and halve the tomatoes. Add to the salad bowl with the olives.

To make the dressing, drain the anchovies and put in a blender with the mustard, garlic, olive oil, lemon juice, 2 tablespoons of hot water, and black pepper. Whiz together until smooth and thickened.

To make the croutons, cut the bread into ½-inch cubes. Heat the oil in a skillet, add the bread cubes, and fry for 3 minutes, turning frequently until golden. Remove and drain on a paper towel.

Drizzle half the anchovy dressing over the prepared salad and toss to coat. Arrange the reserved endive and chicory leaves around the edge, then drizzle over the remaining dressing. Scatter over the croutons and serve immediately.

Try this: FOR AN ALTERNATIVE: 306 FOR KIDS: 164

Hot Shrimp Wrapped in Ham

SERVES 4

½ cucumber, peeled
   if preferred
4 ripe tomatoes
12 raw, large shrimp
6 tbsp olive oil

4 garlic cloves, peeled
   and crushed
4 tbsp freshly
   chopped parsley
salt and freshly ground

black pepper
6 slices Parma ham or
   prosciutto, cut in half
4 slices flat Italian bread
4 tbsp dry white wine

Preheat the oven to 350°F. Slice the cucumber and tomatoes thinly, then arrange on four large plates and reserve. Peel the shrimp, leaving the tail shell intact, and remove the thin black vein running down the back.

Whisk together 4 tablespoons of the olive oil, garlic, and chopped parsley in a small bowl, and season to taste with plenty of salt and pepper. Add the shrimp to the mixture and stir until they are well coated. Remove the shrimp, then wrap each one in a piece of ham and secure with a toothpick.

Place the prepared shrimp on a lightly oiled baking sheet or dish with the slices of bread and cook in the preheated oven for 5 minutes.

Remove the shrimp from the oven and spoon the wine over the shrimp and bread. Return to the oven and cook for a further 10 minutes, until piping hot.

Carefully remove the toothpicks and arrange three shrimp rolls on each slice of bread. Place on top of the sliced cucumber and tomatoes and serve immediately.

Try this: FOR AN ALTERNATIVE: 138   FOR KIDS: 180

Crispy Shrimp
with Chinese Dipping Sauce

SERVES 4

1 lb raw, medium-sized
   shrimp, peeled
¼ tsp salt
6 tbsp peanut oil
2 garlic cloves, peeled and
   finely chopped
1-inch piece fresh ginger,
   peeled and finely chopped

1 green chile pepper,
   deseeded and finely
   chopped
4 stems fresh cilantro,
   leaves and stems
   roughly chopped

For the Chinese
   dipping sauce:
3 tbsp dark soy sauce
3 tbsp rice wine vinegar
1 tbsp superfine sugar
2 tbsp chile oil
2 green onions,
   finely shredded

Using a sharp knife, remove the black vein along the back of the shrimp. Sprinkle the shrimp with the salt and let stand for 15 minutes. Pat dry on a paper towel.

Heat a wok or large skillet and add the peanut oil; when hot, add the shrimp and stir-fry in two batches for about 1 minute, or until they turn pink and are almost cooked. Using a slatted spoon, remove the shrimp and keep warm in a low oven.

Drain the oil from the wok, leaving 1 tablespoon. Add the garlic, ginger, and chile pepper, and cook for about 30 seconds. Add the cilantro, return the shrimp, and stir-fry for 1–2 minutes, or until the shrimp are cooked through and the garlic is golden. Turn into a warmed serving dish.

For the dipping sauce, using a fork beat together the soy sauce, rice vinegar, superfine sugar, and chile oil in a small bowl. Stir in the green onions. Serve immediately with the hot shrimp.

Try this: FOR AN ALTERNATIVE: 176   FOR KIDS: 192

Smoked Haddock Rosti

SERVES 4

3 medium potatoes (about 1 lb), peeled and coarsely grated
1 large onion, peeled and coarsely grated
2–3 garlic cloves, peeled and crushed
1 lb smoked haddock
1 tbsp olive oil
salt and freshly ground black pepper
finely grated rind of ½ lemon
1 tbsp freshly chopped parsley
2 tbsp sour cream
mixed lettuce leaves, to garnish
lemon wedges, to serve

Dry the grated potatoes in a clean kitchen towel. Rinse the grated onion thoroughly in cold water, dry in a clean kitchen towel, and add to the potatoes.

Stir the garlic into the potato mixture. Skin the smoked haddock and remove as many of the tiny bones as possible. Cut into thin slices and reserve.

Heat the oil in a nonstick skillet. Add half the potatoes and press well down in the skillet. Season to taste with salt and pepper.

Add a layer of fish and a sprinkling of lemon rind, parsley, and a little black pepper. Top with the remaining potatoes and press down firmly. Cover with a sheet of foil and cook on the lowest heat for 25–30 minutes.

Preheat the broiler 2–3 minutes before the end of cooking time. Remove the foil and place the rosti under the broiler to brown. Turn out onto a warmed serving dish, and serve immediately with spoonfuls of sour cream, lemon wedges, and mixed lettuce leaves.

Try this: FOR AN ALTERNATIVE: 190 FOR KIDS: 194

Fresh Tuna Salad

SERVES 4

8 cups mixed lettuce leaves
12 baby cherry tomatoes,
　　halved lengthways
4 cups arugula, washed
2 tbsp peanut oil
1¼ lb boned tuna steaks,
　　each cut into 4 pieces

2-oz piece fresh
　　Parmesan cheese

For the dressing:
8 tbsp olive oil
grated zest and juice of
　　2 small lemons

1 tbsp whole-grain mustard
salt and freshly ground
　　black pepper

Wash the lettuce leaves, place them in a large salad bowl with the cherry tomatoes and arugula, and reserve.

Heat the wok, then add the oil and heat until almost smoking. Add the tuna, skin-side down, and cook for 4–6 minutes, turning once during cooking, or until cooked and the flesh flakes easily. Remove from the heat and let stand in the juices for 2 minutes before removing.

Meanwhile, make the dressing. Place the olive oil, lemon zest and juices, and mustard in a small bowl or screw-topped jar and whisk or shake until well blended. Season to taste with salt and pepper.

Transfer the tuna to a clean cutting board and flake, then add it to the salad and toss lightly. Using a swivel blade vegetable peeler, peel the piece of Parmesan cheese into shavings. Divide the salad between four large serving plates, drizzle the dressing over the salad, then scatter with the Parmesan shavings.

Try this: FOR AN ALTERNATIVE: 224　FOR KIDS: 254

Tuna Chowder

SERVES 4

2 tsp oil
1 onion, peeled and
    finely chopped
2 sticks of celery, trimmed
    and finely sliced
1 tbsp all-purpose flour

2½ cups milk
7-oz can tuna in water
11-oz can corn kernels in
    water, drained
2 tsp freshly chopped thyme
salt and freshly ground

black pepper
pinch cayenne pepper
2 tbsp freshly
    chopped parsley

Heat the oil in a large, heavy-based saucepan. Add the onion and celery, and gently cook for about 5 minutes, stirring from time to time until the onion is softened.

Stir in the flour and cook for about 1 minute to thicken. Remove the pan from the heat and gradually pour in the milk, stirring throughout.

Add the tuna and its liquid, the drained corn kernels, and the thyme. Mix gently, then bring to a boil. Cover and simmer for 5 minutes. Remove the pan from the heat and season to taste with salt and pepper.

Sprinkle the chowder with the cayenne pepper and chopped parsley. Divide into soup bowls and serve immediately.

 Try this: FOR AN ALTERNATIVE: 54   FOR KIDS: 118

Warm Swordfish Niçoise

SERVES 4

4 swordfish steaks, about
   1-inch thick, weighing
   about 6 oz each
juice of 1 lime
2 tbsp olive oil
salt and freshly ground
   black pepper

14 oz farfalle pasta
2 cups green beans,
   trimmed and cut in half
1 tsp Dijon mustard
2 tsp white wine vinegar
pinch superfine sugar
3 tbsp olive oil

2 medium tomatoes,
   quartered
12–16 pitted black olives
2 medium eggs, hard boiled
   and quartered
8 anchovy fillets, drained
   and cut in half lengthways

Place the swordfish steaks in a shallow dish. Mix the lime juice with the oil, season to taste with salt and pepper, and spoon over the steaks. Turn the steaks to coat them evenly. Cover and place in the refrigerator to marinate for 1 hour.

Bring a large pan of lightly salted water to a boil. Add the pasta and cook according to the package instructions, or until cooked but still firm. Add the green beans about 4 minutes before the end of cooking time.

Mix the mustard, vinegar, and sugar together in a small jug. Gradually whisk in the olive oil to make a thick dressing.

Cook the swordfish in a griddle pan or under a hot preheated broiler for 2 minutes on each side, or until just cooked through; overcooking will make it tough and dry. Remove and cut into ¾-inch chunks.

Drain the pasta and beans thoroughly and place in a large bowl. Pour over the dressing and toss to coat. Add the cooked swordfish, tomatoes, olives, hard-boiled eggs, and anchovy fillets. Gently toss together, taking care not to break up the eggs. Tip into a warmed serving bowl or divide the pasta between individual plates. Serve immediately.

Try this: FOR AN ALTERNATIVE: 210 FOR KIDS: 234

Fried Smelt
with Arugula Salad

SERVES 4

1 lb smelt, fresh
  or frozen
oil, for frying
¾ cup all-purpose
  flour
½ tsp of cayenne pepper

salt and freshly ground
  black pepper

For the salad:
4 cups arugula
6 cherry tomatoes, halved

⅓ cucumber, cut
  into cubes
3 tbsp olive oil
1 tbsp fresh lemon juice
½ tsp Dijon mustard
½ tsp superfine sugar

If the smelt are frozen, thaw completely then wipe dry with a paper towel. Start to heat the oil in a deep-fat fryer. Arrange the fish in a large, shallow dish, and toss well in the flour, cayenne pepper, and salt and pepper.

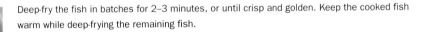

Deep-fry the fish in batches for 2–3 minutes, or until crisp and golden. Keep the cooked fish warm while deep-frying the remaining fish.

Meanwhile, to make the salad, arrange the arugula, cherry tomatoes, and cucumber on individual serving dishes. Whisk the olive oil and the remaining ingredients together, and season lightly. Drizzle the dressing over the salad and serve with the smelt.

Try this: FOR AN ALTERNATIVE: 256   FOR KIDS: 316

Thai Crab Cakes

SERVES 4

1 cup easy-cook basmati rice
2 cups chicken stock, heated
7 oz cooked crab meat
4 oz cod fillet, skinned and ground
5 green onions, trimmed and finely chopped
1 lemon grass stalk, outer leaves discarded and finely chopped
1 green chile pepper, deseeded and finely chopped
1 tbsp freshly grated ginger
1 tbsp freshly chopped cilantro
1 tbsp all-purpose flour
1 medium egg
salt and freshly ground black pepper
2 tbsp vegetable oil, for frying

To serve:
sweet chile dipping sauce
fresh lettuce leaves

Put the rice in a large saucepan and add the hot stock. Bring to a boil, cover, and simmer over a low heat, without stirring, for 18 minutes, or until the grains are tender and all the liquid is absorbed.

To make the cakes, place the crab meat, fish, green onions, lemon grass, chile pepper, ginger, cilantro, flour, and egg in a food processor. Blend until all the ingredients are mixed thoroughly, then season to taste with salt and pepper. Add the rice to the processor and blend once more, but do not over mix.

Remove the mixture from the processor and place on a clean work surface. With damp hands, divide into 12 even-sized patties. Transfer to a plate, cover, and chill in the refrigerator for about 30 minutes.

Heat the oil in a heavy-based skillet and cook the crab cakes, four at a time, for 3–5 minutes on each side until crisp and golden. Drain on a paper towel and serve immediately with a chile dipping sauce.

Try this: FOR AN ALTERNATIVE: 326 FOR KIDS: 324

Seared Scallop Salad

SERVES 4

12 large scallops
1 tbsp margarine
   or butter
2 tbsp orange juice

2 tbsp balsamic vinegar
1 tbsp honey
2 ripe pears, washed
4 cups arugula

4 cups watercress
½ cup walnuts
freshly ground black pepper

Clean the scallops, removing the thin black vein from around the white meat and coral. Rinse thoroughly and dry on a paper towel. Cut into two to three thick slices, depending on the scallop size.

Heat a griddle pan or heavy-based skillet; when hot, add the margarine or butter and let it melt. Once melted, sear the scallops for 1 minute on each side, or until golden. Remove from the pan and reserve.

Briskly whisk together the orange juice, balsamic vinegar, and honey to make the dressing and reserve. With a small, sharp knife carefully cut the pears into quarters, core them, then cut into chunks.

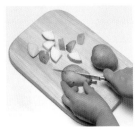

Mix the arugula, watercress, pear chunks, and walnuts. Pile onto serving plates and top with the scallops. Drizzle over the dressing and grind over plenty of black pepper. Serve immediately.

Try this: FOR AN ALTERNATIVE: 352 FOR KIDS: 136

Potato Pancakes with Smoked Salmon

SERVES 4

3 medium floury potatoes
(about 1 lb), peeled and
quartered
salt and freshly ground
black pepper
1 large egg
1 large egg yolk

2 tbsp butter
3 tbsp all-purpose flour
⅔ cup heavy cream
2 tbsp freshly
chopped parsley
5 tbsp sour cream
1 tbsp horseradish sauce

8 oz smoked salmon sliced
lettuce leaves, to serve

To garnish:
lemon slices
snipped chives

Cook the potatoes in a saucepan of lightly salted boiling water for 15–20 minutes, or until tender. Drain thoroughly, then mash until free of lumps. Beat in the whole egg and egg yolk, together with the butter, until smooth and creamy. Slowly beat in the flour and cream, then season to taste with salt and pepper. Stir in the chopped parsley.

Beat the sour cream and horseradish sauce together in a small bowl, cover with plastic wrap, and reserve.

Heat a lightly oiled, heavy-based skillet over a medium-high heat. Place a few spoonfuls of the potato mixture in the hot skillet and cook for 4–5 minutes, or until golden, turning halfway through the cooking time. Remove from the skillet, drain on a paper towel, and keep warm. Repeat with the remaining mixture.

Arrange the pancakes on individual serving plates. Place the smoked salmon on the pancakes and spoon over a little of the horseradish sauce. Serve with salad and the remaining horseradish sauce, and garnish with lemon slices and chives.

Try this: FOR AN ALTERNATIVE: 126 FOR KIDS: 138

Smoked Mackerel Vol–au–Vents

SERVES 1-2

12 oz store-bought puff pastry	mackerel, skinned and chopped	1 tbsp freshly chopped dill
1 small egg, beaten	2-inch piece cucumber	1 tbsp finely grated lemon rind
2 tsp sesame seeds	4 tbsp cream cheese	dill sprigs, to garnish
8 oz peppered smoked	2 tbsp cranberry sauce	mixed lettuce leaves, to serve

Preheat the oven to 450°F. Roll the pastry out on a lightly floured surface and, using a 3½-inch fluted cutter, cut out 12 rounds. Using a ½-inch cutter, mark a lid in the center of each round. Place on a damp baking sheet and brush the rounds with a little beaten egg.

Sprinkle the pastry with the sesame seeds and bake in the preheated oven for 10–12 minutes, or until golden brown and well risen. Transfer the vol-au-vents to a cutting board; when cool enough to touch, carefully remove the lids with a small sharp knife.

Scoop out any uncooked pastry from the inside of each vol-au-vent, then return to the oven for 5–8 minutes to dry out. Remove and let cool.

Flake the mackerel into small pieces and reserve. Peel the cucumber if you want, dice it, and add to the mackerel.

Beat the cream cheese with the cranberry sauce, dill, and lemon rind. Stir in the mackerel and cucumber and use to fill the vol-au-vents. Place the lids on top and garnish with dill sprigs.

Try this: FOR AN ALTERNATIVE: 252   FOR KIDS: 380

Smoked Salmon Sushi

SERVES 4

¾ cup sushi rice
2 tbsp rice vinegar
4 tsp superfine sugar
½ tsp salt

2 sheets sushi nori
2½ oz smoked salmon
¼ cucumber, cut into
    fine strips

To serve:
wasabi
soy sauce
pickled ginger

Rinse the rice thoroughly in cold water, until the water runs clear, then place in a pan with 1¼ cups of water. Bring to a boil and cover with a tight-fitting lid. Reduce to a simmer and cook gently for 10 minutes. Turn the heat off, but keep the pan covered to allow the rice to steam for a further 10 minutes.

In a small saucepan, gently heat the rice vinegar, sugar, and salt until the sugar has dissolved. When the rice has finished steaming, pour over the vinegar mixture and stir well to mix. Empty the rice out onto a large flat surface – a cutting board or large plate is ideal. Fan the rice to cool and give a shinier finish.

Lay one sheet of sushi nori on a sushi mat. If you do not have a sushi mat, improvize with a stiff piece of fabric that is a little larger than the sushi nori. Spread with half the cooled rice – dampen your hands first to prevent the rice from sticking to your fingers. On the nearest edge of the sushi nori place half the salmon and half the cucumber strips.

Using the sushi mat to help you get started, roll up the rice and smoked salmon into a tight, Swiss roll-like shape. Dampen the blade of a sharp knife and cut the sushi into slices about ¾-inch thick. Repeat with the remaining sushi nori, rice, smoked salmon, and cucumber. Serve with wasabi, soy sauce, and pickled ginger.

Try this: FOR AN ALTERNATIVE: 140   FOR KIDS: 132

Thai Fish Cakes

SERVES 4

1 red chile pepper, deseeded and roughly chopped
4 tbsp roughly chopped fresh cilantro
1 garlic clove, peeled and crushed
2 green onions, trimmed

and roughly chopped
1 lemon grass, outer leaves discarded and roughly chopped
3 oz shrimp, thawed if frozen
10 oz cod fillet, skinned, bones removed

and cubed
salt and freshly ground black pepper
sweet chile dipping sauce, to serve

Preheat the oven to 375°F. Place the chile pepper, cilantro, garlic, green onions, and lemon grass in a food processor and blend together.

Pat the shrimp and cod dry with a paper towel. Add to the food processor and blend until the mixture is roughly chopped. Season to taste with salt and pepper and blend to mix.

Dampen your hands, then shape heaped tablespoons of the mixture into 12 little patties. Place the patties on a lightly oiled baking sheet and cook in the preheated oven for 12–15 minutes, or until piping hot and cooked through. Turn the patties over halfway through the cooking time.

Serve the fish cakes immediately with the sweet chile sauce for dipping.

Try this: FOR AN ALTERNATIVE: 144   FOR KIDS: 372

Quick Mediterranean Shrimp

SERVES 4

20 raw Mediterranean
  shrimp
3 tbsp olive oil
1 garlic clove, peeled
  and crushed
finely grated zest and juice
  of ½ lemon

sprigs of fresh rosemary

For the pesto & sun-dried
  tomato dips:
⅔ cup plain yogurt
1 tbsp store-bought pesto
⅔ cup sour cream

1 tbsp sun-dried
  tomato paste
1 tbsp whole-grain mustard
salt and freshly ground
  black pepper
lemon wedges, to garnish

Remove the shells from the shrimp, leaving the tail shells attached. Using a small, sharp knife, remove the dark vein that runs along the back of the shrimp. Rinse and drain on a paper towel.

Whisk 2 tablespoons of the oil with the garlic, lemon zest, and juice in a small bowl. Bruise one sprig of rosemary with a rolling pin and add to the bowl. Add the shrimp, toss to coat, then cover and let marinate in the refrigerator until needed.

For the simple dips, mix the yogurt and pesto in one bowl and the sour cream, tomato paste, and mustard in another bowl. Season to taste with salt and pepper.

Heat a wok, add the remaining oil and swirl round to coat the sides. Remove the shrimp from the marinade, leaving any juices and the rosemary behind. Add to the wok and stir-fry over a high heat for 3–4 minutes, or until the shrimp are pink and just cooked through.

Remove the shrimp from the wok and arrange on a platter. Garnish with lemon wedges and more fresh rosemary sprigs and serve hot or cold with the dips.

Smoked Salmon Quiche

SERVES 6

2 cups all-purpose flour
4 tbsp butter
4 tbsp white vegetable
  fat or lard
2 tsp sunflower oil
1–2 potatoes, peeled
  and diced

1 cup Gruyere
  cheese, grated
3 oz smoked
  salmon trimmings
5 medium eggs, beaten
⅔ cup light cream
salt and freshly ground

black pepper
1 tbsp freshly chopped flat-
  leaf parsley

To serve:
mixed lettuce leaves
baby new potatoes

Preheat the oven to 400°F. Blend the flour, butter, and white vegetable fat or lard together until it resembles fine bread crumbs. Blend again, adding enough water to make a firm but pliable dough. Use the dough to line a 9-inch tart pan or pie pan, then chill the pie shell in the refrigerator for 30 minutes. Fill the shell with dried beans or rice to weigh it down and bake for 10 minutes.

Heat the oil in a small skillet, add the diced potato, and cook for 3–4 minutes, until lightly browned. Reduce the heat and cook for 2–3 minutes, or until tender. Let cool.

Scatter the grated cheese evenly over the bottom of the pie shell, then arrange the cooled potato on top. Add the smoked salmon in an even layer.

Beat the eggs with the cream and season to taste with salt and pepper. Whisk in the parsley and pour the mixture carefully into the pan over the salmon and potato.

Reduce the oven to 350°F and bake for about 30–40 minutes, or until the filling is set and golden. Serve hot or cold with a mixed salad and baby new potatoes.

Mediterranean Feast

SERVES 4

1 small iceberg lettuce
½ cup green beans
5–6 baby new potatoes
    (about 8 oz), scrubbed
4 medium eggs
1 green bell pepper
1 medium onion, peeled
7-oz can tuna, drained and
    flaked into small pieces
½ cup hard cheese,

such as Edam,
    cut into small cubes
8 ripe but firm cherry
    tomatoes, quartered
10–12 black pitted
    olives, halved
freshly chopped basil,
    to garnish

For the lime vinaigrette:
3 tbsp light olive oil
2 tbsp white wine vinegar
4 tbsp lime juice
grated rind of 1 lime
1 tsp Dijon mustard
1–2 tsp superfine sugar
salt and freshly ground
    black pepper

Cut the lettuce into four and remove the hard core. Tear into bite-sized pieces and arrange on a large serving platter or four individual plates.

Cook the green beans in boiling salted water for 8 minutes and the potatoes for 10 minutes, or until tender. Drain and rinse in cold water until cool, then cut both the beans and potatoes in half with a sharp knife.

Boil the eggs for 10 minutes, then rinse thoroughly under cold running water until cool. Remove the shells under the water and cut each egg into four.

Remove the seeds from the pepper and cut it into thin strips; finely chop the onion. Arrange the beans, potatoes, eggs, peppers, and onion on top of the lettuce. Add the tuna, cheese, and tomatoes. Sprinkle over the olives and garnish with the basil.

To make the vinaigrette, place all the ingredients in a screw-topped jar and shake vigorously until everything is mixed thoroughly. Spoon 4 tablespoons over the top of the prepared salad and serve the remainder separately.

Try this: FOR AN ALTERNATIVE: 238   FOR KIDS: 202

Smoked Mackerel & Potato Salad

SERVES 4

½ tsp dry mustard powder
1 large egg yolk
salt and freshly ground
  black pepper
⅔ cup sunflower oil
1–2 tbsp lemon juice

9–12 baby new potatoes
  (about 1 lb)
2 tbsp butter
12 oz smoked mackerel
  fillets
4 celery stalks, trimmed

  and finely chopped
3 tbsp creamed horseradish
⅔ cup sour cream
1 small head lettuce, rinsed
  and roughly torn
8 cherry tomatoes, halved

Place the mustard powder and egg yolk in a small bowl with salt and pepper and whisk until blended. Add the oil, drop by drop, into the egg mixture, whisking continuously. When the mayonnaise is thick, add the lemon juice, drop by drop, until a smooth, glossy consistency is achieved. Reserve.

Cook the potatoes in boiling salted water until tender, then drain. Cool slightly, then cut into halves or quarters, depending on their size. Return to the saucepan and toss in the butter.

Remove the skin from the mackerel fillets and flake into pieces. Add to the potatoes in the saucepan, together with the celery.

Blend 4 tablespoons of the mayonnaise with the horseradish and sour cream. Season to taste with salt and pepper, then add to the potato and mackerel mixture and stir lightly.

Arrange the lettuce and tomatoes on four serving plates. Pile the smoked mackerel mixture on top of the lettuce, grind over a little pepper, and serve with the remaining mayonnaise.

Try this: FOR AN ALTERNATIVE: 282   FOR KIDS: 328

Honey & Ginger Shrimp

SERVES 4

1 carrot
2 oz bamboo shoots
4 green onions
1 tbsp clear honey
1 tbsp ketchup
1 tsp soy sauce
1-inch piece fresh ginger,
    peeled and finely grated

1 garlic clove, peeled
    and crushed
1 tbsp lime juice
6 oz peeled shrimp, thawed
    if frozen
2 small heads lettuce
2 tbsp freshly
    chopped cilantro

salt and freshly ground
    black pepper

To garnish:
fresh cilantro sprigs
lime slices

Cut the carrot into matchstick-sized pieces, roughly chop the bamboo shoots, and finely slice the green onions. Combine the bamboo shoots with the carrot matchsticks and green onions.

In a wok or large skillet, gently heat the honey, ketchup, soy sauce, ginger, garlic, and lime juice with 3 tablespoons of water. Bring to a boil.

Add the carrot mixture and stir-fry for 2–3 minutes, until the vegetables are hot. Add the shrimp and continue to stir-fry for 2 minutes. Remove the wok or skillet from the heat and reserve until cooled slightly.

Divide the lettuce heads into leaves and rinse lightly. Stir the chopped cilantro into the shrimp mixture and season to taste with salt and pepper. Spoon onto the lettuce leaves and serve immediately garnished with sprigs of fresh cilantro and lime slices.

Rice with Smoked Salmon & Ginger

SERVES 4

1¼ cups basmati rice
2½ cups fish stock
1 bunch green onions, trimmed and diagonally sliced
3 tbsp freshly

chopped cilantro
1 tsp grated fresh ginger
7 oz sliced smoked salmon
2 tbsp soy sauce

1 tsp sesame oil
2 tsp lemon juice
4–6 slices pickled ginger
2 tsp sesame seeds
arugula, to serve

Place the rice in a sieve and rinse under cold water until the water runs clear. Drain, then place in a large saucepan with the stock and bring gently to a boil. Reduce to a simmer and cover with a tight-fitting lid. Cook for 10 minutes, then remove from the heat and let stand, covered, for a further 10 minutes.

Stir the green onions, cilantro, and fresh ginger into the cooked rice and mix well. Spoon the rice into four tartlet pans, each measuring 4 inches, and press down firmly with the back of a spoon to form cakes. Invert a pan onto an individual serving plate, then tap the bottom firmly and remove the pan. Repeat with the rest of the filled pans.

Top the rice with the salmon, folding if necessary, so the sides of the rice can still be seen in places. Mix together the soy sauce, sesame oil, and lemon juice to make a dressing, then drizzle over the salmon. Top with the pickled ginger and a sprinkling of sesame seeds. Scatter the arugula around the edge of the plates and serve immediately.

Try this: FOR AN ALTERNATIVE: 126 FOR KIDS: 122

Citrus Monkfish Kebabs

SERVES 4

For the marinade:
1 tbsp sunflower oil
finely grated rind and juice
  of 1 lime
1 tbsp lemon juice
1 sprig of freshly
  chopped rosemary

1 tbsp whole-grain mustard
1 garlic clove, peeled
  and crushed
salt and freshly ground
  black pepper

For the kebabs:
1 lb monkfish tail
8 raw, large shrimp
1 small zucchini, trimmed
  and sliced
4 tbsp sour cream

Preheat the broiler and line the broiler rack with foil. Mix all the marinade ingredients together in a small bowl and reserve.

Using a sharp knife, cut down both sides of the monkfish tail. Remove the bone and discard. Cut away and discard any skin, then cut the monkfish into bite-sized cubes.

Peel the shrimp, leaving the tails intact, and remove the thin black vein that runs down the back of each shrimp. Place the fish and shrimp in a shallow dish.

Pour the marinade over the fish and shrimp. Cover lightly and let marinate in the refrigerator for 30 minutes. Spoon the marinade over the fish and shrimp occasionally during this time. Soak the skewers in cold water for 30 minutes, then drain.

Thread the cubes of fish, shirmp, and zucchini onto the drained skewers. Arrange on the broiler rack, then place under the preheated broiler and cook for 5–7 minutes, or until cooked thoroughly and the shrimp have turned pink. Occasionally brush with the remaining marinade and turn the kebabs during cooking. Mix 2 tablespoons of the marinade with the sour cream and serve as a dip with the kebabs.

Try this: FOR AN ALTERNATIVE: 296   FOR KIDS: 170

Salmon Fish Cakes

SERVES 4

1–2 potatoes (about 8 oz), peeled
1 lb salmon fillet, skinned
1–2 carrots (about 4 oz), trimmed and peeled
2 tbsp grated lemon rind
2–3 tbsp freshly

chopped cilantro
1 medium egg yolk
salt and freshly ground black pepper
2 tbsp all-purpose flour
few fine sprays of oil

To serve:
ketchup
tossed green salad
crusty bread

Cube the potatoes and cook in lightly salted, boiling water for 15 minutes. Drain and mash the potatoes. Place in a mixing bowl and reserve.

Place the salmon in a food processor and blend to form a chunky puree. Add the puree to the potatoes and mix together. Coarsely grate the carrot and add to the fish with the lemon rind and the cilantro.

Add the egg yolk, season to taste with salt and pepper, then gently mix the ingredients together. With damp hands, form the mixture into four large fish cakes. Coat in the flour and place on a plate. Cover loosely and chill for at least 30 minutes.

When ready to cook, spray a griddle pan with a few fine sprays of oil and heat the pan. When hot, add the fish cakes and cook on both sides for 3–4 minutes, or until the fish is cooked. Add an extra spray of oil if needed during the cooking.

When the fish cakes are cooked, serve immediately with the ketchup, green salad, and crusty bread.

Try this: FOR AN ALTERNATIVE: 118 FOR KIDS: 324

Mediterranean Chowder

SERVES 6

1 tbsp olive oil
1 tbsp butter
1 large onion, peeled and finely sliced
4 celery stalks, trimmed and thinly sliced
2 garlic cloves, peeled and crushed
1 bird's-eye chile pepper, deseeded and finely chopped
1 tbsp all-purpose flour
1–2 medium potatoes (about 8 oz), peeled and diced
2½ cups fish or vegetable stock
1½ lb whiting or cod fillet, cut into 1-inch cubes
2 tbsp freshly chopped parsley
4 oz large, peeled shrimp
7-oz can corn kernels, drained
salt and freshly ground black pepper
⅔ cup light cream
1 tbsp freshly snipped chives
warm crusty bread, to serve

Heat the oil and butter together in a large saucepan, add the onion, celery, and garlic, and cook gently for 2–3 minutes, until softened. Add the chile pepper and stir in the flour. Cook, stirring, for a further minute.

Add the potatoes to the saucepan with the stock. Bring to a boil, cover, and simmer for 10 minutes. Add the fish cubes to the saucepan with the chopped parsley and cook for a further 5–10 minutes, or until the fish and potatoes are just tender.

Stir in the peeled shrimp and corn kernels, and season to taste with salt and pepper. Pour in the cream and adjust the seasoning, if necessary.

Scatter the snipped chives over the top of the chowder. Ladle into six large bowls and serve immediately with plenty of warm crusty bread.

Try this: FOR AN ALTERNATIVE: 112   FOR KIDS: 62

Chef's Rice Salad

SERVES 4

1¼ cups wild rice
½ cucumber
10 cherry tomatoes
6 green onions, trimmed
5 tbsp extra virgin olive oil
2 tbsp balsamic vinegar
1 tsp Dijon mustard

1 tsp superfine sugar
salt and freshly ground
black pepper
4 cups arugula
4 oz lean bacon
4 oz cooked chicken
meat, finely diced

1 cup Swiss cheese, grated
4 oz large cooked shrimp,
peeled
1 avocado, pitted, peeled,
and sliced, to garnish
warm crusty bread, to serve

Put the rice in in a saucepan of water and bring to a boil, stirring once or twice. Reduce the heat, cover, and simmer gently for 30–50 minutes, depending on the texture you prefer. Drain well and reserve.

Thinly peel the cucumber, cut in half, then using, a teaspoon, remove the seeds. Cut the cucumber into thin slices. Cut the tomatoes in quarters. Cut the green onions into diagonal slices.

Whisk the olive oil with the vinegar, then whisk in the mustard and sugar. Season to taste with salt and pepper. In a large bowl, gently toss together the cooled rice with the tomatoes, cucumber, green onions, and arugula. Pour over the dressing and toss lightly together.

Heat a griddle pan; when hot, cook the bacon on both sides for 4–6 minutes, or until crisp. Remove and chop. Arrange the prepared salad on a platter, then arrange the bacon, chicken, cheese, and shrimp on top. Toss if you want. Garnish with the avocado slices and serve with plenty of warm crusty bread.

Try this: FOR AN ALTERNATIVE: 162 FOR KIDS: 280

Curly Endive & Seafood Salad

SERVES 4

1 head (of) curly
   endive lettuce
2 green bell peppers
5-inch piece cucumber
4 oz squid, cleaned and cut
   into thin rings
16 baby asparagus spears
4 oz smoked salmon slices,
   cut into wide strips

16 oz fresh, cooked mussels
   in their shells

For the lemon dressing:
2 tbsp sunflower oil
1 tbsp white wine vinegar
5 tbsp fresh lemon juice
1–2 tsp superfine sugar
1 tsp whole-grain mustard

salt and freshly ground
   black pepper

To garnish:
slices of lemon
sprigs of fresh cilantro

Rinse and tear the endive into small pieces and arrange on a serving platter. Remove the seeds from the bell peppers and cut the peppers and the cucumber into small cubes. Sprinkle over the endive.

Bring a saucepan of water to a boil and add the squid rings. Bring the pan to a boil again, then switch off the heat and let stand for 5 minutes. Drain and rinse thoroughly in cold water.

Cook the asparagus in boiling water for 5 minutes, or until tender but just crisp. Arrange with the squid, smoked salmon, and mussels on top of the salad.

To make the lemon dressing, put all the ingredients into a screw-topped jar, or into a small bowl, and mix thoroughly until the ingredients are combined.

Spoon 3 tablespoons of the dressing over the salad and serve the remainder in a small jug. Garnish the salad with slices of lemon and sprigs of cilantro and serve.

Try this: FOR AN ALTERNATIVE: 222   FOR KIDS: 224

Scallop & Potato Gratin

SERVES 4

8 fresh scallops in their
    shells, cleaned
4 tbsp white wine
salt and freshly ground
    black pepper

4 tbsp butter
3 tbsp all-purpose flour
2 tbsp light cream
½ cup Cheddar
    cheese, grated

3 medium potatoes
    (about 1 lb), peeled
    and cut into chunks
1 tbsp milk

Preheat the oven to 425°F. Clean four scallop shells to use as serving dishes and reserve. Place the scallops in a small saucepan with the wine, ⅔ cup of water, and salt and pepper. Cover and simmer gently for 5 minutes, or until just tender. Remove with a slatted spoon and cut each scallop into three pieces. Reserve the cooking juices for the next step.

Melt 2 tablespoons of the butter in a saucepan, stir in the flour, and cook for 1 minute, stirring, then gradually whisk in the reserved cooking juices. Simmer, stirring, for 3–4 minutes, until the sauce has thickened. Season to taste with salt and pepper. Remove from the heat and stir in the cream and half of the grated cheese. Fold in the scallops.

Boil the potatoes in lightly salted water until tender, then mash with the remaining butter and milk. Spoon or pipe the mashed potato around the edges of the cleaned scallop shells.

Divide the scallop mixture between the four shells, placing the mixture neatly in the center. Sprinkle with the remaining grated cheese and bake in the preheated oven for about 10–15 minutes, until golden brown and bubbling. Serve immediately.

 Try this: FOR AN ALTERNATIVE: 120 FOR KIDS: 264

Salmon & Phyllo Parcels

SERVES 4

1 tbsp sunflower oil
1 bunch of green onions,
    trimmed and
    finely chopped
1 tsp paprika
1 cup long-grain
    white rice

⅔ cup fish stock
salt and freshly ground
    black pepper
1 lb salmon
    fillet, cubed
1 tbsp freshly
    chopped parsley

grated rind and juice
    of 1 lemon
5 cups arugula
5 cups spinach
12 sheets phyllo dough
4 tbsp butter, melted

Preheat the oven to 400°F. Heat the oil in a small skillet and gently cook the green onions for 2 minutes. Stir in the paprika and cook for 1 minute, then remove from the heat and reserve.

Put the rice in a sieve and rinse under cold running water until the water runs clear, then drain. Put the rice and stock in a saucepan, bring to a boil, then cover and simmer for 10 minutes, or until the liquid is absorbed and the rice is tender. Add the green onion mixture and fork through. Season to taste with salt and pepper, then let cool. In a nonmetallic bowl, mix together the salmon, parsley, lemon rind and juice, and salt and pepper. Reserve.

Blanch the arugula and spinach for 30 seconds in a large saucepan of boiling water, or until just wilted. Drain well in a colander and refresh in plenty of cold water, then squeeze out as much moisture as possible.

Brush three sheets of phyllo dough with melted butter and lay them on top of one another. Take one-quarter of the rice mixture and arrange it in an oblong in the center of the dough. On top of this place one-quarter of the salmon, followed by one-quarter of the arugula and spinach. Draw up the dough around the filling and twist at the top to create a parcel. Repeat with the remaining dough and filling until you have four parcels. Brush with the remaining butter. Place on a lightly oiled baking sheet and cook in the preheated oven for 20 minutes, or until golden brown and cooked. Serve immediately.

Supreme Baked Potatoes

SERVES 4

4 large baking potatoes
3 tbsp butter
1 tbsp sunflower oil
1 carrot, peeled
   and chopped

2 celery stalks, trimmed and
   finely chopped
7-oz can white crab meat
2 green onions, trimmed
   and finely chopped

salt and freshly ground
   black pepper
½ cup Cheddar
   cheese, grated
tomato salad, to serve

Preheat the oven to 400°F. Scrub the potatoes and prick all over with a fork, or thread two potatoes onto two long metal skewers. Place the potatoes in the preheated oven for 1–1½ hours, or until soft to the touch. Let cool a little, then cut in half.

While the potatoes are cooking, heat the oil in a skillet and cook the carrot and celery for 2 minutes. Cover the pan tightly and continue to cook for another 5 minutes, or until the vegetables are tender.

Scoop out the cooked potato and turn into a bowl, leaving a reasonably firm potato shell. Mash the cooked potato flesh, then mix in the butter and mash until the butter has melted.

Add the cooked vegetables to the bowl of mashed potato and mix well. Fold in the crab meat and the green onions, then season to taste with salt and pepper.

Pile the mixture back into the potato shells and press in firmly. Sprinkle the grated cheese over the top and return the potato halves to the oven for 12–15 minutes, until hot, golden, and bubbling. Serve immediately with a tomato salad.

Try this: FOR AN ALTERNATIVE: 218   FOR KIDS: 180

Scallops & Monkfish Kebabs with Fennel Sauce

SERVES 4

1½ lb monkfish tail
8 large fresh scallops
2 tbsp olive oil
1 garlic clove, peeled
    and crushed
freshly ground black pepper
1 fennel bulb, trimmed and

thinly sliced
assorted lettuce leaves,
    to serve

For the sauce:
2 tbsp fennel seeds
pinch of chile flakes

4 tbsp olive oil
2 tsp lemon juice
salt and freshly ground
    black pepper

Place the monkfish on a cutting board and remove the skin and the bone that runs down the center of the tail and discard. Lightly rinse and pat dry with a paper towel. Cut the two fillets into 12 equal-sized pieces and place in a shallow bowl. Remove the scallops from their shells, if necessary, and clean thoroughly, discarding the black vein. Rinse lightly and pat dry with a paper towel. Put in the bowl with the fish.

Blend the 2 tablespoons of olive oil, the crushed garlic, and a pinch of black pepper in a small bowl, then pour the mixture over the monkfish and scallops, making sure they are well coated. Cover lightly and leave to marinate in the refrigerator for at least 30 minutes, or longer if time permits. Spoon over the marinade occasionally.

Lightly crush the fennel seeds and chile flakes in a pestle and mortar. Stir in the olive oil and lemon juice and season to taste with salt and pepper. Cover and let infuse for 20 minutes. Drain the monkfish and scallops, reserving the marinade and thread onto four skewers. Spray a griddle pan with a fine spray of oil, then heat until almost smoking and cook the kebabs for 5–6 minutes, turning halfway through and brushing with the marinade throughout. Brush the fennel slices with the fennel sauce and cook on the griddle for 1 minute on each side. Serve the fennel slices, topped with the kebabs and drizzled with the fennel sauce. Serve with a few assorted lettuce leaves.

Try this: FOR AN ALTERNATIVE: 142   FOR KIDS: 296

Sardines in Vine Leaves

SERVES 4

8–16 grape leaves in
brine, drained
2 green onions
6 tbsp olive oil
2 tbsp lime juice
2 tbsp freshly
chopped oregano

1 tsp mustard powder
salt and freshly ground
black pepper
8 sardines, cleaned
8 bay leaves
8 sprigs of fresh dill

To garnish:
lime wedges
sprigs of fresh dill

To serve:
olive salad
crusty bread

Preheat the broiler and line the broiler rack with tinfoil just before cooking. Cut eight pieces of string about 10 inches long, and let soak in cold water for about 10 minutes. Cover the vine leaves in almost boiling water. Let stand for 20 minutes, then drain and rinse thoroughly. Pat the vine leaves dry with a paper towel.

Trim the green onions and finely chop, then place them into a small bowl. With a wire whisk, beat in the olive oil, lime juice, oregano, and mustard powder, and season to taste with salt and pepper. Cover with plastic wrap and reserve in the refrigerator until required. Stir the mixture before using.

Prepare the sardines by making two slashes on both sides of each fish and brushing with a little of the lime juice mixture. Place a bay leaf and a dill sprig inside each sardine cavity and wrap with 1–2 vine leaves, depending on their size. Brush with the lime mixture and tie the vine leaves in place with string.

Grill the fish for 4–5 minutes on each side under a medium heat, brushing with a little more of the lime mixture if necessary. Leave the fish to rest, unwrap, and discard the vine leaves. Garnish with lime wedges and sprigs of fresh dill, and serve with the remaining lime mixture, olive salad, and crusty bread.

Try this: FOR AN ALTERNATIVE: 116   FOR KIDS: 144

Marinated Mackerel with Tomato & Basil Salad

SERVES 3

3 mackerel, filleted
3 beefsteak tomatoes, sliced
2 cups watercress
2 oranges, peeled
    and segmented
¾ cup mozzarella
    cheese, sliced
2 tbsp basil leaves,

shredded
sprig of fresh basil,
    to garnish

For the marinade:
juice of 2 lemons
4 tbsp olive oil
4 tbsp basil leaves

For the dressing:
1 tbsp lemon juice
1 tsp Dijon mustard
1 tsp superfine sugar
salt and freshly ground
    black pepper
5 tbsp olive oil

Remove as many of the fine bones as possible from the mackerel fillets, lightly rinse, and pat dry with a paper towel and place in a shallow dish.

Blend the marinade ingredients together and pour over the mackerel fillets. Make sure the marinade covers the fish completely. Cover and let stand in a cool place for at least 8 hours, but preferably overnight. As the fillets marinate, they will lose their translucency and look as if they are cooked.

Place the tomatoes, watercress, oranges, and mozzarella cheese in a large bowl and toss. To make the dressing, whisk the lemon juice with the mustard, sugar, olive oil and seasoning in a bowl. Pour over half the dressing, toss again, and then arrange on a serving platter.

Remove the mackerel from the marinade, cut into bite-sized pieces, and sprinkle with the shredded basil. Arrange on top of the salad, drizzle over the remaining dressing, scatter with basil leaves, and garnish with a basil sprig. Serve.

Try this: FOR AN ALTERNATIVE: 136   FOR KIDS: 266

Sesame Shrimp Toast

SERVES 4

4 oz peeled, cooked shrimp
1 tbsp cornstarch
2 green onions, peeled and
   roughly chopped
2 tsp freshly grated ginger
2 tsp dark soy sauce

pinch of Chinese five spice
   powder (optional)
1 small egg, beaten
salt and freshly ground
   black pepper
6 thin slices day-old

white bread
5 tbsp sesame seeds
vegetable oil for deep-frying
chile sauce, to serve

Place the shrimp in a food processor or blender with the cornstarch, green onions, ginger, soy sauce, and Chinese five spice powder, if using. Blend to a fairly smooth paste. Spoon into a bowl and stir in the beaten egg. Season to taste with salt and pepper.

Cut the crusts off the bread. Spread the shrimp paste in an even layer on one side of each slice. Sprinkle over the sesame seeds and press down lightly.

Cut each slice diagonally into four triangles. Place on a board and chill in the refrigerator for 30 minutes.

Pour sufficient oil into a heavy-based saucepan or deep-fat fryer so that it is one-third full. Heat until it reaches a temperature of 350°F. Cook the toasts in batches of five or six, carefully lowering them seeded-side down into the oil. Deep-fry for 2–3 minutes, or until lightly browned, then turn over and cook for 1 minute more. Using a slatted spoon, lift out the toast and drain on a paper towel. Keep warm while frying the remaining toast. Arrange on a warmed platter and serve immediately with some chile sauce for dipping.

Try this: FOR AN ALTERNATIVE: 192   FOR KIDS: 194

Appetizers: Meat

Sweet & Sour Spareribs

SERVES 4

3½ lb pork spareribs
4 tbsp clear honey
1 tbsp Worcestershire sauce
1 tsp Chinese five
    spice powder

4 tbsp soy sauce
2½ tbsp dry sherry
1 tsp chile sauce
2 garlic cloves, peeled
    and chopped

1½ tbsp tomato paste
1 tsp dry mustard
    powder (optional)
green onion curls,
    to garnish

Preheat the oven to 400°F 15 minutes before cooking. If necessary, place the ribs on a cutting board and, using a sharp knife, cut the joint inbetween the ribs, to form single ribs. Place the ribs in a shallow dish in a single layer.

Add the honey, Worcestershire sauce, and Chinese five spice powder with the soy sauce, sherry, and chile sauce to a small saucepan and heat gently, stirring until smooth. Stir in the chopped garlic, the tomato paste, and mustard powder, if using.

Pour the honey mixture over the ribs and spoon over until the ribs are coated evenly. Cover with plastic wrap and let marinate overnight in the refrigerator, occasionally spooning the marinade over the ribs.

When ready to cook, remove the ribs from the marinade and place in a shallow roasting pan. Spoon over a little of the marinade and reserve the remainder. Place the spareribs in the preheated oven and cook for 35–40 minutes, or until cooked and the outsides are crisp. Baste occasionally with the reserved marinade during cooking. Garnish with a few green onion curls and serve immediately, either as an appetizer or as a meat accompaniment.

Try this: FOR AN ALTERNATIVE: 200   FOR KIDS: 184

Mixed Satay Sticks

SERVES 4

12 large, raw shrimp
12 oz beef rump steak
1 tbsp lemon juice
1 garlic clove, peeled
   and crushed
salt
2 tsp dark brown sugar
1 tsp ground cumin

1 tsp ground coriander
¼ tsp ground turmeric
1 tbsp groundnut oil
fresh cilantro leaves,
   to garnish

For the spicy peanut sauce:
⅔ cup coconut milk

1 shallot, peeled and
   finely chopped
1 tsp granulated sugar
pinch of chile powder
1 tbsp dark soy sauce
½ cup crunchy
   peanut butter

Preheat the broiler on high just before required. Soak eight bamboo skewers in cold water for at least 30 minutes. Peel the shrimp, leaving the tails on. Using a sharp knife, remove the black vein along the back of the shrimp. Cut the beef into ½-inch wide strips. Place the shrimp and beef in separate bowls and sprinkle each with ½ tablespoon of the lemon juice. Mix together the garlic, pinch of salt, sugar, cumin, coriander, turmeric, and groundnut oil to make a paste. Lightly brush over the shrimp and beef. Cover and place in the refrigerator to marinate for at least 30 minutes, but for longer if possible.

Meanwhile, make the sauce. Pour the coconut milk into a small saucepan, add the shallot, sugar, and soy sauce and heat gently until the sugar has dissolved. Stir in the chile powder. When melted, remove from the heat and stir in the peanut butter. Let cool slightly, then spoon into a serving dish.

Thread three shrimp each onto four skewers and divide the sliced beef between the remaining skewers. Cook the skewers under the preheated broiler for 4–5 minutes, turning occasionally. The shrimp should be opaque and pink and the beef browned on the outside, but still pink in the center. Transfer to warmed individual serving plates, garnish with a few fresh cilantro leaves and serve immediately with the warm peanut sauce.

Try this: FOR AN ALTERNATIVE: 100   FOR KIDS: 218

Spicy Beef Pancakes

SERVES 4

½ cup all-purpose flour
pinch of salt
½ tsp Chinese five
   spice powder
1 large egg yolk
⅔ cup milk
4 tsp sunflower oil
slices of green onion,
   to garnish

For the spicy beef filling:
1 tbsp sesame oil
4 green onions, sliced
½ inch piece fresh ginger,
   peeled and grated
1 garlic clove, peeled
   and crushed
11 oz sirloin steak, trimmed
   and cut into strips

1 red chile pepper, deseeded
   and finely chopped
1 tsp sherry vinegar
1 tsp dark brown sugar
1 tbsp dark soy sauce

Sift the flour, salt, and Chinese five spice powder into a bowl and make a well in the center. Add the egg yolk and a little of the milk. Gradually beat in, drawing in the flour to make a smooth batter. Whisk in the rest of the milk. Heat 1 teaspoon of the sunflower oil in a small, heavy-based skillet. Pour in just enough batter to thinly coat the bottom of the skillet. Cook over a medium heat for 1 minute, or until the underside of the pancake is golden brown.

Turn or toss the pancake and cook for 1 minute, or until the other side of the pancake is golden brown. Make seven more pancakes with the remaining batter. Stack them on a warmed plate as you make them, with greaseproof paper between each pancake. Cover with foil and keep warm in an oven on a low setting.

To make the filling, heat a wok or large skillet and add the sesame oil; when hot, add the green onions, ginger, and garlic, and stir-fry for 1 minute. Add the beef strips, stir-fry for 3–4 minutes, then stir in the chile pepper, vinegar, sugar, and soy sauce. Cook for 1 minute, then remove from the heat. Spoon one-eighth of the filling over one-half of each pancake. Fold the pancakes in half, then fold in half again. Garnish with a few slices of green onion and serve immediately.

Try this: FOR AN ALTERNATIVE: 230 FOR KIDS: 264

Swedish Cocktail Meatballs

SERVES 4-6

4 tbsp butter
1 onion, peeled and
 finely chopped
1 cup fresh white
 bread crumbs
1 medium egg, beaten

½ cup heavy cream
salt and freshly ground
 black pepper
12 oz fresh lean ground beef
4 oz fresh ground pork
3–4 tbsp freshly chopped dill

½ tsp ground allspice
1 tbsp vegetable oil
½ cup beef stock
cream cheese and chives,
 or cranberry sauce,
 to serve

Heat half the butter in a large wok, add the onion, and cook, stirring frequently, for 4–6 minutes, or until softened and beginning to color. Transfer to a bowl and let cool. Wipe out the wok with a paper towel.

Add the bread crumbs and beaten egg with 1–2 tablespoons of cream to the softened onion. Season to taste with salt and pepper and stir until well blended. Using your fingertips, crumble the ground beef and pork into the bowl. Add half the dill and all of the allspice and, using your hands, mix together until well blended. With dampened hands, shape the mixture into 1-inch balls.

Melt the remaining butter in the wok and add the vegetable oil, swirling it to coat the side of the wok. Working in batches, add about one-quarter to one-third of the meatballs in a single layer and cook for 5 minutes, swirling and turning until golden and cooked. Transfer to a plate and continue with the remaining meatballs, transferring them to the plate as they are cooked.

Pour off the fat in the wok. Add the beef stock and bring to a boil, then boil until reduced by half, stirring and scraping up any browned bits from the bottom. Add the remaining cream and continue to simmer until slightly thickened and reduced. Stir in the remaining dill and season if necessary. Add the meatballs and simmer for 2–3 minutes, or until heated right through. Serve with toothpicks, with the cream cheese or cranberry sauce in a separate bowl for dipping.

Try this: FOR AN ALTERNATIVE: 204 FOR KIDS: 228

Dim Sum Pork Parcels

MAKES ABOUT 40

4-oz can water chestnuts, drained and finely chopped
4 oz raw shrimp, peeled, deveined, and coarsely chopped
12 oz fresh ground pork
2 tbsp smoked bacon, finely chopped
1 tbsp light soy sauce, plus extra, to serve
1 tsp dark soy sauce
1 tbsp Chinese rice wine
2 tbsp fresh ginger, peeled and finely chopped
3 green onions, trimmed and finely chopped
2 tsp sesame oil
1 medium egg white, lightly beaten
salt and freshly ground black pepper
2 tsp sugar
40 wonton skins, thawed if frozen
toasted sesame seeds, to garnish
soy sauce, to serve

Place the water chestnuts, shrimp, ground pork, and bacon in a bowl and mix together. Add the soy sauces, Chinese rice wine, ginger, chopped green onion, sesame oil, and egg white. Season to taste with salt and pepper, sprinkle in the sugar, and mix the filling thoroughly.

Place a spoonful of filling in the center of a wonton skin. Bring the sides up and press around the filling to make a basket shape. Flatten the base of the skin, so the wonton stands solid. The top should be wide open, exposing the filling.

Place half the parcels on a heatproof plate, on a wire rack inside a wok or on the bottom of a muslin-lined bamboo steamer. Place over a wok, half-filled with boiling water, cover, then steam the parcels for about 20 minutes. Repeat for the second batch. Transfer to a warmed serving plate, sprinkle with toasted sesame seeds, drizzle with soy sauce, and serve immediately.

Try this: FOR AN ALTERNATIVE: 192   FOR KIDS: 194

Moo Shui Pork

SERVES 4

6 oz pork fillet
2 tsp Chinese rice wine
   or dry sherry
2 tbsp light soy sauce
1 tsp cornstarch
1 oz dried golden needles,
   soaked and drained
2 tbsp peanut oil

3 medium eggs,
   lightly beaten
1 tsp freshly grated ginger
3 spring onions, trimmed
   and thinly sliced
5 oz bamboo shoots, cut
   into fine strips
salt and freshly ground

black pepper
8 mandarin
   pancakes, steamed
hoisin sauce
sprigs of fresh cilantro,
   to garnish

Cut the pork across the grain into ½-inch slices, then cut into thin strips. Place in a bowl with the Chinese rice wine or sherry, soy sauce, and cornstarch. Mix well and reserve. Trim off the tough ends of the golden needles, then cut in half and reserve.

Heat a wok or large skillet and add 1 tablespoon of the peanut oil; when hot, add the lightly beaten eggs and cook for 1 minute, stirring all the time, until scrambled. Remove and reserve. Wipe the wok clean with a paper towel.

Return the wok to the heat and add the remaining oil; when hot, transfer the pork strips from the marinade mixture to the wok, shaking off as much marinade as possible. Stir-fry for 30 seconds, then add the ginger, spring onions, and bamboo shoots and pour in the marinade. Stir-fry for 2–3 minutes or until cooked.

Return the scrambled eggs to the wok, season to taste with salt and pepper, and stir for a few seconds until mixed well and heated through. Divide the mixture between the pancakes, drizzle each with 1 teaspoon of hoisin sauce, and roll up. Garnish and serve immediately.

Try this: FOR AN ALTERNATIVE: 326   FOR KIDS: 256

Potato Skins

SERVES 4

4 large baking potatoes
2 tbsp olive oil
2 tsp paprika,
4 oz pancetta, roughly
   chopped

6 tbsp heavy cream
1 cup Gorgonzola cheese
1 tbsp freshly
   chopped parsley

To serve:
mayonnaise
sweet chile dipping sauce
tossed green salad
paprika, to garnish

Preheat the oven to 400°F. Scrub the potatoes, then prick a few times with a fork or skewer and place directly on the top shelf of the oven. Bake in the preheated oven for at least 1 hour, or until tender. The potatoes are cooked when they yield gently to the pressure of your hand.

Set the potatoes aside until cool enough to handle, then cut in half and scoop the flesh into a bowl and reserve. Preheat the broiler and line the broiler rack with foil.

Mix together the oil and paprika, and use half to brush the outside of the potato skins. Place on the broiler rack under the preheated hot broiler and cook for 5 minutes, or until crisp, turning as necessary.

Heat the remaining paprika-flavored oil and gently fry the pancetta until crisp. Add to the potato flesh, along with the cream, Gorgonzola cheese, and parsley. Halve the potato skins and fill with the Gorgonzola filling. Return to the oven for a further 15 minutes to heat through. Sprinkle with a little more paprika and serve immediately with mayonnaise, sweet chile sauce, and a green salad.

Try this: FOR AN ALTERNATIVE: 188   FOR KIDS: 260

Bacon, Mushroom, & Cheese Puffs

SERVES 4

1 tbsp olive oil
3¼ cups mushrooms, cleaned and roughly chopped
8 oz bacon, roughly chopped
2 tbsp freshly chopped parsley
salt and freshly ground black pepper
12 oz phyllo dough, thawed if frozen
¼ cup Swiss cheese, grated
1 medium egg, beaten
arugula or watercress, to garnish
tomatoes, to serve

Preheat the oven to 400°F. Heat the olive oil in a large skillet. Add the mushrooms and bacon and fry for 6–8 minutes until golden in color. Stir in the parsley, season to taste with salt and pepper, and let cool.

Roll the phyllo dough a little thinner on a lightly floured surface to a 12-inch square. Cut the dough into four equal squares.

Stir the grated Swiss cheese into the mushroom mixture. Spoon one-quarter of the mixture on to one half of each square. Brush the edges of the square with a little of the beaten egg.

Fold over the dough to form a triangular parcel. Seal the edges well and place on a lightly oiled baking sheet. Repeat until the squares are done.

Make shallow slashes in the top of the parcels with a knife. Brush the parcels with the remaining beaten egg and cook in the preheated oven for 20 minutes, or until puffy and golden brown. Serve warm or cold, garnished with the arugula or watercress, and served with tomatoes.

Try this: FOR AN ALTERNATIVE: 252 FOR KIDS: 316

Oven–baked Pork Balls with Peppers

SERVES 4

For the garlic bread:
2–4 garlic cloves, peeled
4 tbsp butter, softened
1 tbsp freshly
    chopped parsley
2–3 tsp lemon juice
1 focaccia loaf

For the pork balls:
1 lb fresh ground pork

4 tbsp freshly chopped basil
2 garlic cloves, peeled
    and chopped
3 sundried
    tomatoes, chopped
salt and freshly ground
    black pepper
3 tbsp olive oil
1 medium red bell pepper,
    deseeded and cut

into chunks
1 medium green bell pepper,
    deseeded and cut into
    chunks
1 medium yellow bell
    pepper, deseeded and
    cut into chunks
12–14 cherry tomatoes
2 tbsp balsamic vinegar

Preheat the oven to 400°F 15 minutes before cooking. Crush the garlic, then blend with the softened butter, the parsley, and enough lemon juice to give a soft consistency. Shape into a roll, wrap in baking parchment paper, and chill in the refrigerator for at least 30 minutes.

Mix together the pork, basil, 1 chopped garlic clove, sundried tomatoes, and seasoning until well combined. With damp hands, divide the mixture into 16, roll into balls, and reserve. Spoon the olive oil into a large roasting pan and place in the preheated oven for about 3 minutes, until hot. Remove from the heat and stir in the pork balls, the remaining chopped garlic, and the bell peppers. Bake for about 15 minutes. Remove from the oven, stir in the cherry tomatoes, and season to taste with plenty of salt and pepper. Bake for about a further 20 minutes.

Just before the pork balls are ready, slice the bread, toast lightly, and spread with the prepared garlic butter. Remove the pork balls from the oven, stir in the vinegar, and serve immediately with the garlic bread.

Try this: FOR AN ALTERNATIVE: 334 FOR KIDS: 174

Crispy Pork with Tangy Sauce

SERVES 4

12 oz pork fillet
1 tbsp light soy sauce
1 tbsp dry sherry
salt and freshly ground
   black pepper
1 tbsp sherry vinegar
1 tbsp tomato paste

1 tbsp dark soy sauce
2 tsp light brown sugar
⅔ cup chicken stock
1½ tsp clear honey
8 tsp cornstarch
2 cups peanut oil
   for frying

1 medium egg

To garnish:
fresh sprigs of dill
orange wedges

Remove and discard any fat and sinew from the pork fillet, cut into ¾-inch cubes, and place in a shallow dish. Blend the light soy sauce with the dry sherry and add seasoning. Pour over the pork and stir until the pork is lightly coated. Cover and let marinate in the refrigerator for at least 30 minutes, stirring occasionally.

Meanwhile, blend the sherry vinegar, tomato paste, dark soy sauce, light brown sugar, chicken stock, and honey together in a small saucepan. Heat gently, stirring occasionally until the sugar has dissolved, then bring to a boil.

Blend 2 teaspoons of cornstarch with 1 tablespoon of water and stir into the sauce. Cook, stirring, until smooth and thickened, and either keep warm or reheat when required.

Heat the oil in the wok to 375°F. Whisk together the remaining 6 teaspoons of cornstarch and the egg to make a smooth batter. Drain the pork if necessary, then dip the pieces into the batter, allowing any excess to drip back into the bowl. Cook in the hot oil for 2–3 minutes, or until golden and tender. Drain on a paper towel. Cook the pork in batches until it is all cooked, then garnish and serve immediately with the sauce.

Crispy Baked Potatoes
with Serrano Ham

SERVES 4

4 large baking potatoes
4 tsp crème fraîche or
   sour cream
salt and freshly ground
   black pepper
2 oz lean serrano ham or

prosciutto, with
   fat removed
½ cup cooked fava beans
⅓ cup cooked carrots,
   diced
⅓ cup cooked peas

½ cup hard cheese,
   such as Edam or
   Cheddar, grated
fresh green salad, to serve

Preheat the oven to 400°F. Scrub the potatoes dry. Prick with a fork and place on a baking sheet. Cook for 1–1½ hours or until tender when squeezed. Use oven mitts or a kitchen towel to pick up the potatoes – they will be hot.

Cut the potatoes in half horizontally and scoop out all the flesh into a bowl. Spoon the crème fraîche into the bowl and mix thoroughly with the potatoes. Season to taste with a little salt and pepper.

Cut the ham into strips and carefully stir into the potato mixture with the fava beans, carrots, and peas. Pile the mixture back into the eight potato shells and sprinkle a little grated cheese on top of each.

Place under a hot broiler and cook until golden and heated through. Serve immediately with a fresh green salad.

Try this: FOR AN ALTERNATIVE: 190   FOR KIDS: 136

Special Rosti

SERVES 4

4–5 medium potatoes
(about 1½ lb), scrubbed
but not peeled
salt and freshly ground
black pepper
6 tbsp butter
1 large onion, peeled and

finely chopped
1 garlic clove, peeled
and crushed
2 tbsp freshly
chopped parsley
1 tbsp olive oil
3 oz Parma ham or

prosciutto, thinly sliced
20 sundried tomatoes
(about 2 oz), chopped
1½ cups Swiss cheese,
grated
mixed green salad, to serve

Cook the potatoes in a large saucepan of salted boiling water for about 10 minutes, until just tender. Drain in a colander, then rinse in cold water. Drain again. Let cool enough to handle, then peel off the skins.

Melt the butter in a large skillet and gently fry the onion and garlic for about 3 minutes, until softened and beginning to color. Remove from the heat. Coarsely grate the potatoes into a large bowl, then stir in the onion and garlic mixture. Sprinkle over the parsley and stir well to mix. Season to taste with salt and pepper.

Heat the oil in the skillet and cover the bottom of the pan with half the potato mixture. Lay the slices of Parma ham on top. Sprinkle with the chopped sundried tomatoes, then scatter the grated cheese over the top.

Finally, top with the remaining potato mixture. Cook over a low heat, pressing down with a spatula from time to time, for 10–15 minutes, or until the bottom is golden brown. Carefully invert the rosti onto a large plate, then carefully slide back into the pan and cook the other side until golden. Serve cut into wedges, with a mixed green salad.

Try this: FOR AN ALTERNATIVE: 108   FOR KIDS: 132

Crispy Pork Wontons

SERVES 4

1 small onion, peeled and roughly chopped
2 garlic cloves, peeled and crushed
1 green chile pepper, deseeded and chopped
1-inch piece fresh ginger, peeled and roughly chopped
1 lb lean ground pork
4 tbsp freshly chopped cilantro
1 tsp Chinese five spice powder
salt and freshly ground black pepper
20 wonton wrappers
1 medium egg, lightly beaten
vegetable oil for deep-frying
chile sauce, to serve

Place the onion, garlic, chile pepper, and ginger in a food processor and blend until finely chopped. Add the pork, cilantro, and Chinese five spice powder. Season to taste with salt and pepper, then blend again briefly to mix. Divide the mixture into 20 equal portions and, with floured hands, shape each into a walnut-sized ball.

Brush the edges of a wonton wrapper with beaten egg, place a pork ball in the center, then bring the corners to the center and pinch together to make a parcel. Repeat with the remaining pork balls and wrappers.

Pour sufficient oil into a heavy-based saucepan or deep-fat fryer so that it is one-third full and heat to 350˚F. Deep-fry the wontons in three or four batches for 3–4 minutes, or until cooked through and golden and crisp. Drain on a paper towel. Serve the crispy pork wontons immediately, allowing five per person, with some chile sauce for dipping.

Try this: FOR AN ALTERNATIVE: 326   FOR KIDS: 286

Egg Rolls

MAKES 26–30 ROLLS

For the filling:
½ oz dried shiitake
mushrooms
2 oz rice vermicelli
1–2 tbsp peanut oil
1 small onion, peeled and
finely chopped
3–4 garlic cloves, peeled and
finely chopped
1½-inch piece fresh ginger,
peeled and chopped

8 oz fresh ground pork
2 green onions, trimmed
and finely chopped
¾ cup bean sprouts
4 water chestnuts, chopped
2 tbsp freshly
snipped chives
6 oz cooked shrimp, peeled
and chopped
1 tsp oyster sauce
1 tsp soy sauce

salt and freshly ground
black pepper
green onion tassels,
to garnish

For the wrappers:
4–5 tbsp all-purpose flour
26–30 egg roll wrappers
1¼ cups vegetable oil for
deep frying

Soak the shiitake mushrooms in almost boiling water for 20 minutes. Remove and squeeze out the liquid. Discard any stems, slice, and reserve. Soak the rice vermicelli as per the package instructions. Heat a large wok and add the oil; when hot, add the onion, garlic, and ginger and stir-fry for 2 minutes. Add the pork, green onions, and shiitake mushrooms and stir-fry for 4 minutes. Stir in the bean sprouts, water chestnuts, chives, shrimp, oyster sauce, and soy sauce. Season to taste with salt and pepper and spoon into a bowl. Drain the noodles well, add to the bowl, and toss until well mixed, then let cool.

Blend the flour to a smooth paste with 3–4 tablespoons of water. Soften a wrapper in a plate of warm water for 1–2 seconds, then drain. Put 2 tablespoons of the filling near one edge of the wrapper, fold the edge over the filling, then fold in each side and roll up. Seal with a little flour paste and transfer to a baking sheet, seam-side down. Repeat with the remaining wrappers. Heat the oil in a large wok to 375°F, or until a cube of bread browns in 30 seconds. Fry the egg rolls a few at a time, until golden. Remove and drain on a paper towel. Arrange on a serving plate and garnish with green onion tassels. Serve immediately.

Try this: FOR AN ALTERNATIVE: 308 FOR KIDS: 380

Barbecue Pork Steamed Rolls

SERVES 12

For the rolls:
1½–1¾ cups all-purpose flour
1 tbsp dried yeast
½ cup milk
2 tbsp sunflower oil
1 tbsp sugar
½ tsp salt
spring gren onion curls,
    to garnish

fresh green lettuce
    leaves, to serve

For the filling:
2 tbsp vegetable oil
1 small red bell pepper,
    deseeded and
    finely chopped
2 garlic cloves, peeled and

finely chopped
8 oz cooked pork, finely
    chopped
¼ cup light brown sugar
¼ cup ketchup
1–2 tsp hot chile powder,
    or to taste

Put ¾ cup of the flour in a bowl and stir in the yeast. Heat the milk, oil, sugar, and salt in a small saucepan until warm, stirring until the sugar has dissolved. Pour into the bowl and, with an electric mixer, beat on a low speed for 30 seconds, scraping down the sides of the bowl, until blended. Beat at high speed for 3 minutes, then with a wooden spoon stir in as much of the remaining flour as possible, until a stiff dough forms. Shape into a ball, place in a lightly oiled bowl, cover with plastic wrap, and let stand for 1 hour in a warm place, or until doubled in size. To make the filling, heat a wok and add the oil; when hot, add the red bell pepper and garlic. Stir-fry for 4–5 minutes. Add the remaining ingredients and bring to a boil, stir-frying for 2–3 minutes, until thick and syrupy. Cool and reserve.

Punch down the dough and turn onto a lightly floured surface. Divide into 12 pieces and shape them into balls, then cover and let stand for 5 minutes. Roll each ball into a 3-inch circle. Place a heaped tablespoon of filling in the center of each. Dampen the edges, then bring them up around the filling, pinching together to seal. Place seam-side down on a small square of nonstick baking paper. Continue with the remaining dough and filling. Let rise for 10 minutes. Bring a large wok half-filled with water to a boil and place the rolls in a lightly oiled Chinese steamer. Cover and steam for 20–25 minutes, then remove and cool slightly. Garnish with green onion tassels and serve with lettuce leaves.

Try this: FOR AN ALTERNATIVE: 262 FOR KIDS: 366

Appetizers: Poultry

Soy-glazed Chicken Thighs

SERVES 6-8

2 lb chicken thighs
2 tbsp vegetable oil
3-4 garlic cloves, peeled
   and crushed
1½-inch piece fresh ginger,
   peeled and finely

chopped or grated
½ cup soy sauce
2-3 tbsp Chinese rice wine
   or dry sherry
2 tbsp clear honey
1 tbsp brown sugar

2-3 dashes hot chile sauce,
   or to taste
freshly chopped parsley,
   to garnish

Heat a large wok and add the oil; when hot, stir-fry the chicken thighs for 5 minutes, or until golden. Remove and drain on a paper towel. You may need to do this in 2–3 batches.

Pour off the oil and fat and, using a paper towel, carefully wipe out the wok. Add the garlic, ginger, soy sauce, Chinese rice wine or sherry, and honey to the wok and stir well. Sprinkle in the brown sugar with the hot chile sauce to taste, then place over the heat and bring to a boil.

Reduce the heat to a gentle simmer, then carefully add the chicken thighs. Cover the wok and simmer gently over a low heat for 30 minutes, or until they are tender and the sauce is reduced and thickened and glazes the chicken thighs.

Occasionally stir or spoon the sauce over the chicken thighs, and add a little water if the sauce starts to become too thick. Arrange in a shallow serving dish, garnish with freshly chopped parsley, and serve immediately.

Try this: FOR AN ALTERNATIVE: 228   FOR KIDS: 168

Chicken & Pasta Salad

SERVES 6

1 lb pasta
2–3 tbsp extra virgin olive oil
11 oz cold cooked chicken
   (preferably roasted), cut
   into bite-sized pieces
1 red bell pepper, deseeded
   and diced
1 yellow bell pepper,
   deseeded and diced
4–5 sundried tomatoes,

sliced
2 tbsp capers, rinsed
   and drained
28–30 pitted large
   black olives
4 green onions, chopped
2 cups mozzarella cheese,
   diced
salt and freshly ground
   black pepper

For the dressing:
¼ cup red or white
   wine vinegar
1 tbsp mild mustard
1 tsp sugar
⅓–½ cup extra virgin olive oil
½ cup mayonnaise

Bring a large saucepan of lightly salted water to a boil. Add the pasta and cook for 10 minutes, or until cooked but firm. Drain the pasta and rinse under cold running water, then drain again. Place in a large serving bowl and toss with the olive oil.

Add the chicken, diced red and yellow bell peppers, sliced sundried tomatoes, capers, olives, green onions, and mozzarella cheese to the pasta, and toss gently until mixed. Season to taste with salt and pepper.

To make the dressing, put the vinegar, mustard, and sugar into a small bowl or jug, and whisk until well blended and the sugar is dissolved. Season with some pepper, then gradually whisk in the olive oil in a slow, steady stream, until a thickened vinaigrette forms.

Place the mayonnaise in a bowl and gradually whisk in the dressing until smooth. Pour over the pasta mixture and mix gently until all the ingredients are coated. Turn into a large, shallow serving bowl and serve at room temperature.

Try this: FOR AN ALTERNATIVE: 102   FOR KIDS: 320

Cilantro Chicken & Soy Sauce Cakes

SERVES 4

¼ cucumber, peeled
1 shallot, peeled and
    thinly sliced
6 radishes, trimmed
    and sliced
12 oz skinless, boneless
    chicken thigh

4 tbsp roughly chopped
    fresh cilantro
2 green onions, trimmed
    and roughly chopped
1 red chile pepper, deseeded
    and chopped
finely grated rind of ½ lime

2 tbsp soy sauce
1 tbsp superfine sugar
2 tbsp rice vinegar
1 red chile pepper, deseeded
    and finely sliced
freshly chopped cilantro,
    to garnish

Preheat the oven to 375°F. Halve the cucumber lengthwise, deseed, and dice. In a bowl, mix the shallot and radishes. Chill until ready to serve with the diced cucumber.

Place the chicken thighs in a food processor and blend until coarsely chopped. Add the cilantro and green onions to the chicken with the chile pepper, lime rind, and soy sauce. Blend again until mixed.

Using slightly damp hands, shape the chicken mixture into 12 small rounds. Place the rounds on a lightly oiled baking sheet and bake in the preheated oven for 15 minutes, until golden.

In a small pan, heat the sugar with 2 tablespoons of water until dissolved. Simmer until syrupy. Remove from the heat and let cool a little, then stir in the vinegar and slices of chile pepper.

Pour over the cucumber and the radish and shallot salad. Garnish with the chopped cilantro and serve the chicken cakes with the salad immediately.

Try this: FOR AN ALTERNATIVE: 118 FOR KIDS: 184

Crostini with Chicken Livers

SERVES 4

2 tbsp olive oil
2 tbsp butter
1 shallot, peeled and
   finely chopped
1 garlic clove, peeled
   and crushed
5 oz chicken livers
1 tbsp all-purpose flour

2 tbsp dry white wine
1 tbsp brandy
¾ cup mushrooms, sliced
salt and freshly ground
   black pepper
4 slices of ciabatta or
   similar bread

To garnish:
fresh sage leaves
lemon wedges

Heat 1 tablespoon of the olive oil and 1 tablespoon of the butter in a skillet, add the shallot and garlic, and cook gently for 2–3 minutes.

Trim and wash the chicken livers thoroughly and pat dry on a paper towel as much as possible. Cut into slices, then toss in the flour. Add the livers to the skillet with the shallot and garlic and continue to fry for a further 2 minutes, stirring continuously.

Pour in the white wine and brandy and bring to a boil. Boil rapidly for 1–2 minutes to let the alcohol evaporate, then stir in the sliced mushrooms and cook gently for about 5 minutes, or until the chicken livers are cooked but just a little pink inside. Season to taste with salt and pepper.

Fry the slices of ciabatta or similar style bread in the remaining oil and butter, then place on individual serving dishes. Spoon over the liver mixture and garnish with a few sage leaves and lemon wedges. Serve immediately.

Try this: FOR AN ALTERNATIVE: 258   FOR KIDS: 324

Oriental Chicken on Arugula & Tomato

SERVES 4

2 shallots, peeled	12 oz fresh ground chicken	1 tbsp fish sauce
1 garlic clove, peeled	1 tsp Chinese	8 cherry tomatoes
1 carrot, peeled	five spice powder	2 cups arugula
½ cup water chestnuts	pinch chile powder	
1 tsp oil	1 tsp soy sauce	

Finely chop the shallots and garlic. Cut the carrot into matchsticks, thinly slice the water chestnuts, and reserve. Heat the oil in a wok or heavy-based large skillet and add the chicken. Stir-fry for 3–4 minutes over a moderately high heat, breaking up any large pieces of chicken.

Add the garlic and shallots and cook for 2–3 minutes, until softened. Sprinkle over the Chinese five spice powder and the chile powder and continue to cook for about 1 minute.

Add the carrot, water chestnuts, soy sauce, fish sauce, and 2 tablespoons of water. Stir-fry for a further 2 minutes. Remove from the heat and reserve to cool slightly.

Deseed the tomatoes and cut into thin wedges. Toss with the arugula and divide between four serving plates. Spoon the warm chicken mixture over the arugula and tomato wedges and serve immediately to prevent the arugula from wilting.

Try this: FOR AN ALTERNATIVE: 138   FOR KIDS: 196

Wild Rice & Bacon Salad with Smoked Chicken

SERVES 4

1 cup wild rice
½ cup pecan or
    walnut halves
1 tbsp vegetable oil
4 slices smoked
    bacon, diced

3–4 shallots, peeled and
    finely chopped
⅓ cup walnut oil
2–3 tbsp sherry or
    cider vinegar
2 tbsp freshly chopped dill

salt and freshly ground
    black pepper
10 oz smoked chicken or
    duck breast, thinly sliced
dill sprigs, to garnish

Put the wild rice in a medium saucepan with 2½ cups of water and bring to a boil, stirring once or twice. Reduce the heat, cover, and simmer gently for 30–50 minutes, depending on the texture you prefer, chewy or tender. Using a fork, gently fluff into a large bowl and let cool slightly.

Meanwhile, toast the nuts in a skillet over a medium heat for 2 minutes, or until they are fragrant and lightly colored, stirring and tossing frequently. Cool, then chop coarsely and add to the rice.

Heat the oil in the skillet over a medium heat. Add the bacon and cook, stirring from time to time, for 3–4 minutes, or until crisp and brown. Remove from the pan and drain on a paper towel. Add the shallots to the skillet and cook for 4 minutes, or until just softened, stirring from time to time. Stir into the rice and nuts, with the drained bacon pieces.

Whisk the walnut oil, vinegar, half the dill, and the salt and pepper in a small bowl until combined. Pour the dressing over the rice mixture and toss well to combine. Mix the chicken and the remaining chopped dill into the rice, then spoon into bowls and garnish each serving with a dill sprig. Serve slightly warm, or at room temperature.

Try this: FOR AN ALTERNATIVE: 162   FOR KIDS: 234

Rice & Papaya Salad

SERVES 4

¾ cup easy-cook basmati rice
1 cinnamon stick, crushed
1 bird's-eye chile pepper, deseeded and finely chopped
rind and juice of 2 limes
rind and juice of 2 lemons
2 tbsp Thai fish sauce

1 tbsp light brown sugar
1 papaya, peeled and seeds removed
1 mango, peeled and stone removed
1 green chile pepper, deseeded and finely chopped

2 tbsp freshly chopped cilantro
1 tbsp freshly chopped mint
9 oz cooked chicken
⅛ cup roasted peanuts, chopped
strips of pita bread, to serve

Rinse and drain the rice and pour into a saucepan. Add 2 cups of boiling salted water and the cinnamon stick. Bring to a boil, reduce the heat to a low level, cover, and cook, without stirring, for 15–18 minutes, or until all the liquid is absorbed. The rice should be light and fluffy and have steam holes on the surface. Remove the cinnamon stick and stir in the rind from 1 lime.

To make the dressing, place the bird's-eye chile pepper, remaining rind and lime and lemon juice, fish sauce, and sugar in a food processor, and mix for a few minutes until blended. Alternatively, place all these ingredients in a screw-top jar and shake until well blended. Pour half the dressing over the hot rice and toss until the rice glistens.

Slice the papaya and mango into thin slices, then place in a bowl. Add the chopped green chile pepper, cilantro, and mint. Place the chicken on a cutting board, then remove and discard any skin or sinews. Cut into fine shreds and add to the bowl with the chopped peanuts.

Add the remaining dressing to the chicken mixture and stir until all the ingredients are lightly coated. Spoon the rice onto a platter, pile the chicken mixture on top, and serve with strips of warm pita bread.

Try this: FOR AN ALTERNATIVE: 306   FOR KIDS: 270

Sweet & Sour Rice with Chicken

SERVES 4

4 green onions	1 garlic clove, peeled	4 tbsp ketchup
2 tsp sesame oil	and crushed	1 tbsp tomato paste
1 tsp Chinese	1 medium onion, peeled and	2 tbsp honey
five spice powder	sliced into thin wedges	1 tbsp vinegar
1 lb chicken breast,	1½ cups long-grain	1 tbsp dark soy sauce
cut into cubes	white rice	1 carrot, peeled and cut
1 tbsp oil	2½ cups water	into matchsticks

Trim the green onions, then cut lengthways into fine strips. Drop into a large bowl of iced water and reserve.

Mix together the sesame oil and Chinese five spice powder, and rub the mixture into the cubed chicken. Heat the wok and add the oil; when hot, cook the garlic and onion for 2–3 minutes, or until transparent and softened.

Add the chicken and stir-fry over a medium-high heat until the chicken is golden and cooked through. Using a slatted spoon, remove from the wok and keep warm.

Stir the rice into the wok and add the water, ketchup, tomato paste, honey, vinegar, and soy sauce. Stir well to mix. Bring to a boil, then simmer until almost all of the liquid is absorbed. Stir in the carrot and reserved chicken, and continue to cook for 3–4 minutes.

Drain the green onions, which will have become curly. Garnish with the green onion curls and serve immediately with the rice and chicken.

Try this: FOR AN ALTERNATIVE: 74 FOR KIDS: 218

Spicy Chicken Skewers with Mango Tabbouleh

SERVES 4

14 oz chicken breast fillet
1 cup plain yogurt
1 garlic clove, peeled
   and crushed
1 small red chile pepper,
   deseeded and finely
   chopped
½ tsp ground turmeric
finely grated rind and juice
   of ½ lemon

sprigs of fresh mint,
   to garnish

For the mango tabbouleh:
1 cup bulgur
1 tsp olive oil
juice of ½ lemon
½ red onion, finely chopped
1 ripe mango, halved,
   stoned, peeled,

   and chopped
¼ cucumber, finely diced
2 tbsp freshly
   chopped parsley
2 tbsp freshly shredded mint
salt and finely ground
   black pepper

If using wooden skewers, presoak them in cold water for at least 30 minutes. This stops them from burning during broiling. Cut the chicken into 2 x ½-inch strips and place in a shallow dish. Mix together the yogurt, garlic, chile pepper, turmeric, and lemon rind and juice. Pour over the chicken and toss to coat. Cover and let marinate in the refrigerator for up to 8 hours.

To make the tabbouleh, put the bulgur in a bowl. Pour over enough boiling water to cover. Put a plate over the bowl and let soak for 20 minutes. Whisk together the oil and lemon juice in a bowl. Add the red onion and leave to marinade for 10 minutes.

Drain the bulgur and squeeze out any excess moisture in a clean kitchen towel. Add to the red onion with the mango, cucumber, and herbs, and season to taste with salt and pepper. Toss together. Thread the chicken strips onto eight wooden or metal skewers. Cook under a hot broiler for 8 minutes. Turn and brush with the marinade, until the chicken is lightly browned and cooked through.

Spoon the tabbouleh onto individual plates. Arrange the chicken skewers on top and garnish with the sprigs of mint. Serve warm or cold.

Try this: FOR AN ALTERNATIVE: 142   FOR KIDS: 296

Chicken & New Potatoes on Rosemary Skewers

SERVES 4

8 thick fresh rosemary
    stems, 9 inches long
3–4 tbsp extra virgin olive oil
2 garlic cloves, peeled
    and crushed
1 tsp freshly chopped thyme
grated rind and juice
    of 1 lemon

salt and freshly ground
    black pepper
4 skinless chicken
    breast fillets
16 small new potatoes,
    peeled or scrubbed
8 very small onions or
    shallots, peeled

1 large yellow or red bell
    pepper, deseeded
lemon wedges, to garnish
parsley-flavored cooked rice,
    to serve

Preheat the broiler and line the broiler rack with foil just before cooking. If using a barbecue, light at least 20 minutes before required. Strip the leaves from the rosemary stems, leaving about 2 inches of soft leaves at the top. Chop the leaves coarsely and reserve. Using a sharp knife, cut the thicker woody ends of the stems to a point that can pierce the chicken pieces and potatoes. Blend the chopped rosemary, oil, garlic, thyme, and lemon rind and juice in a shallow dish. Season to taste with salt and pepper. Cut the chicken into ½-inch cubes, add to the flavored oil, and stir well. Cover and refrigerate for at least 30 minutes, turning occasionally.

Cook the potatoes in lightly salted boiling water for 10–12 minutes, until just tender. Add the onions to the potatoes 2 minutes before the end of the cooking time. Drain, rinse under cold running water, and let cool. Cut the pepper into 1-inch squares. Beginning with a piece of chicken and starting with the pointed end of the skewer, alternately thread equal amounts of chicken, potato, pepper, and onion onto each rosemary skewer. Cover the leafy ends of the skewers with foil to stop them from burning. Do not thread the chicken and vegetables too closely together on the skewer or the chicken may not cook completely.

Cook the kebabs for 15 minutes, or until tender and golden, turning and brushing with either extra oil or the marinade. Remove the foil, garnish with lemon wedges, and serve on rice.

Try this: FOR AN ALTERNATIVE: 158 FOR KIDS: 170

Warm Chicken & Potato Salad with Peas & Mint

SERVES 4-6

9–12 new potatoes
   (about 1 lb), peeled or
   scrubbed and cut into
   bite-sized pieces
salt and freshly ground
   black pepper
2 tbsp cider vinegar
1⅓ cups frozen peas, thawed

1 small ripe avocado
4 cooked chicken breasts
   (about 1 lb), skinned
   and diced
2 tbsp freshly chopped mint
2 small heads lettuce
fresh mint sprigs, to garnish

For the dressing:
2 tbsp raspberry or
   sherry vinegar
2 tsp Dijon mustard
1 tsp clear honey
¼ cup sunflower oil
¼ cup extra virgin olive oil

Cook the potatoes in lightly salted boiling water for 15 minutes, or until just tender when pierced with the tip of a sharp knife; do not overcook. Rinse under cold running water to cool slightly, then drain and turn into a large bowl. Sprinkle with the cider vinegar and toss gently.

Run the peas under hot water to ensure that they are thawed, pat dry with a paper towel, and add to the potatoes.

Cut the avocado in half lengthways and remove the stone. Peel and cut the avocado into cubes and add to the potatoes and peas. Add the chicken and stir together lightly.

To make the dressing, place all the ingredients in a screw-top jar, with a little salt and pepper, and shake well to mix; add a little more oil if the flavor is too strong. Pour over the salad and toss gently to coat. Sprinkle in half the mint and stir lightly.

Separate the lettuce leaves and spread onto a large shallow serving plate. Spoon the salad on top and sprinkle with the remaining mint. Garnish with mint sprigs and serve.

this FOR AN ALTERNATIVE: 212 FOR KIDS: 210

Warm Fruity Rice Salad

SERVES 4

1 cup mixed basmati
   and wild rice
4 oz skinless chicken breast
1¼ cups chicken or vegetable
   stock
⅔ cup dried apricots
⅔ cup dried dates
3 sticks celery

For the dressing:
2 tbsp sunflower oil
1 tbsp white wine vinegar
4 tbsp lemon juice
1–2 tsp clear honey, warmed
1 tsp Dijon mustard
freshly ground black pepper

To garnish:
6 green onions
sprigs of fresh cilantro

Place the rice in a pan of boiling salted water and cook for 15–20 minutes, or until tender. Rinse thoroughly with boiling water and reserve.

Meanwhile wipe the chicken and place in a shallow saucepan with the stock. Bring to a boil, cover, and simmer for about 15 minutes, or until the chicken is cooked thoroughly and the juices run clear. Let the chicken stand in the stock until cool enough to handle, then cut into thin slices.

Chop the apricots and dates into small pieces. Peel any tough membranes from the outside of the celery and dice. Fold the apricots, dates, celery, and sliced chicken into the warm rice.

Make the dressing by whisking all the ingredients together in a small bowl until mixed thoroughly. Pour 2–3 tablespoons over the rice and stir in gently and evenly. Serve the remaining dressing separately.

Trim and chop the green onions and sprinkle over the top of the salad. Garnish with the sprigs of cilantro and serve while still warm.

Pasta & Pepper Salad

SERVES 4

4 tbsp olive oil

1 each red, orange, and yellow bell pepper, deseeded and cut into chunks

1 large zucchini, trimmed and cut into chunks

1 medium eggplant, trimmed and diced

10 oz fusilli pasta

4 plum tomatoes, quartered

1 bunch fresh basil leaves, roughly chopped

2 tbsp pesto

2 garlic cloves, peeled and roughly chopped

1 tbsp lemon juice

8 oz boneless and skinless roasted chicken breast

salt and freshly ground black pepper

1 cup feta cheese, crumbled

crusty bread, to serve

Preheat the oven to 400°F. Spoon the olive oil into a roasting pan and heat in the oven for 2 minutes, or until almost smoking. Remove from the oven, add the peppers, zucchini, and eggplant, and stir until coated. Bake for 30 minutes, or until charred, stirring occasionally.

Bring a large saucepan of lightly salted water to a boil. Add the pasta and cook according to the package instructions, or until cooked but firm. Drain and refresh under cold running water. Drain thoroughly, place in a large salad bowl, and reserve.

Remove the cooked vegetables from the oven and let cool. Add to the cooled pasta, together with the quartered tomatoes, chopped basil leaves, pesto, garlic, and lemon juice. Toss lightly to mix.

Shred the chicken roughly into small pieces and stir into the pasta and vegetable mixture. Season to taste with salt and pepper, then sprinkle the crumbled feta cheese over the pasta and stir gently. Cover the dish and let marinate for 30 minutes, stirring occasionally. Serve the salad with fresh crusty bread.

Try this: FOR AN ALTERNATIVE: 268   FOR KIDS: 374

Spicy Chicken & Pasta Salad

SERVES 6

1 lb pasta shells
2 tbsp butter
1 onion, peeled
   and chopped
2 tbsp mild curry paste
⅔ cup dried apricots,
   chopped

2 tbsp tomato paste
3 tbsp mango chutney
1¼ cups mayonnaise
15-oz can pineapple slices,
   in fruit juice
salt and freshly ground
   black pepper

1 lb skinned and boned
   cooked chicken, cut
   into bite-sized pieces
¼ cup flaked, toasted
   almond slivers
cilantro sprigs, to garnish

Bring a large saucepan of lightly salted water to a boil. Add the pasta shells and cook according to the package instructions, or until cooked but firm. Drain and refresh under cold running water, then drain thoroughly and place in a large serving bowl.

Meanwhile, melt the butter in a heavy-based saucepan, add the onion, and cook for 5 minutes, or until softened. Add the curry paste and cook, stirring, for 2 minutes. Stir in the apricots and tomato paste, then cook for 1 minute. Remove from the heat and let cool.

Blend the mango chutney and mayonnaise together in a small bowl. Drain the pineapple slices, adding 2 tablespoons of the pineapple juice to the mayonnaise mixture; reserve the pineapple slices. Season the mayonnaise to taste with salt and pepper.

Cut the pineapple slices into chunks and stir into the pasta, together with the mayonnaise mixture, curry paste, and cooked chicken pieces. Toss lightly together to coat the pasta. Sprinkle with the almond slivers, garnish with cilantro sprigs, and serve.

Try this: FOR AN ALTERNATIVE: 216   FOR KIDS: 338

Chicken & Lamb Satay

SERVES 4

8 oz skinless,
    boneless chicken
8 oz lean lamb

For the marinade:
1 small onion, peeled and
    finely chopped
2 garlic cloves, peeled
    and crushed
1-inch piece fresh ginger,
    peeled and grated

4 tbsp soy sauce
1 tsp ground coriander
2 tsp dark brown sugar
2 tbsp lime juice
1 tbsp vegetable oil

For the peanut sauce:
1¼ cups coconut milk
4 tbsp crunchy peanut butter
1 tbsp Thai fish sauce
1 tsp lime juice

1 tbsp chile powder
1 tbsp brown sugar
salt and freshly ground
    black pepper

To garnish:
sprigs of fresh cilantro
lime wedges

Preheat the broiler just before cooking. Soak the bamboo skewers for 30 minutes before required. Cut the chicken and lamb into thin strips about 3 inches long and place in two shallow dishes. Blend all the marinade ingredients together, then pour half over the chicken and half over the lamb. Stir until lightly coated, then cover with plastic wrap and let marinate in the refrigerator for at least 2 hours, turning occasionally.

Remove the chicken and lamb from the marinade and thread onto the skewers. Reserve the marinade. Cook under the preheated broiler for 8–10 minutes, or until cooked, turning and brushing with the marinade.

Meanwhile, make the peanut sauce. Blend the coconut milk with the peanut butter, fish sauce, lime juice, chile powder, and sugar. Pour into a saucepan and cook gently for 5 minutes, stirring occasionally, then season to taste with salt and pepper. Garnish with cilantro sprigs and lime wedges and serve the satays with the prepared sauce.

Try this: FOR AN ALTERNATIVE: 354   FOR KIDS: 200

Chicken & Shrimp–stacked Ravioli

SERVES 4

1 tbsp olive oil
1 onion, peeled
    and chopped
1 garlic clove, peeled
    and chopped
1 lb boned and skinned
    cooked chicken, cut into

    large pieces
1 beefsteak tomato,
    deseeded and chopped
⅔ cup dry white wine
⅔ cup heavy cream
9 oz peeled, cooked shrimp,
    thawed if frozen

2 tbsp freshly chopped
    tarragon, plus sprigs
    to garnish
salt and freshly ground
    black pepper
8 pieces fresh lasagne

Heat the olive oil in a large skillet, add the onion and garlic, and cook for 5 minutes, or until softened, stirring occasionally. Add the chicken pieces and fry for 4 minutes, or until heated through, turning occasionally.

Stir in the chopped tomato, wine, and cream and bring to a boil. Lower the heat and simmer for about 5 minutes, or until reduced and thickened. Stir in the shrimp and tarragon, and season to taste with salt and pepper. Heat the sauce through gently.

Meanwhile, bring a large saucepan of lightly salted water to a boil and add two pieces of lasagne. Return to a boil and cook for 2 minutes, stirring gently to avoid sticking. Remove the lasagne from the saucepan using a slatted spoon, and keep warm. Repeat with the remaining lasagne pieces.

Cut each piece of lasagne in half. Place two pieces on each of the warmed plates and divide half of the chicken mixture among them. Top each serving with a second piece of lasagne and divide the remainder of the chicken mixture among them. Top with a final layer of lasagne. Garnish with tarragon sprigs and serve immediately.

Try this: FOR AN ALTERNATIVE: 268   FOR KIDS: 318

Spicy Chicken with
Open Ravioli & Tomato Sauce

SERVES 2-3

2 tbsp olive oil
1 onion, peeled and
    finely chopped
1 tsp ground cumin
1 tsp hot paprika
1 tsp ground cinnamon
6 oz boneless and skinless

chicken breasts, chopped
salt and freshly ground
    black pepper
1 tbsp smooth peanut butter
4 tbsp butter
1 shallot, peeled and
    finely chopped

2 garlic cloves, peeled
    and crushed
14-oz can chopped tomatoes
4 oz fresh egg lasagne
2 tbsp freshly
    chopped cilantro

Heat the olive oil in a skillet, add the onion, and cook gently for 2–3 minutes; then add the cumin, paprika, and cinnamon, and cook for a further 1 minute. Add the chicken, season to taste with salt and pepper, and cook for 3–4 minutes, or until tender. Add the peanut butter and stir until well mixed, and reserve.

Melt the butter in the skillet, add the shallot, and cook for 2 minutes. Add the tomatoes and garlic and season to taste. Simmer gently for 20 minutes, or until thickened, then keep the sauce warm.

Cut each piece of lasagne into six squares. Bring a large saucepan of lightly salted water to a boil. Add the lasagne squares and cook according to the package instructions, about 3–4 minutes, or until cooked but firm. Drain the lasagne pieces, reserve, and keep warm.

Layer the pasta squares with the spicy filling on individual warmed plates. Pour over a little of the hot tomato sauce and sprinkle with chopped cilantro. Serve immediately.

Try this: FOR AN ALTERNATIVE: 216   FOR KIDS: 226

Turkey & Oven–roasted Vegetable Salad

SERVES 4

6 tbsp olive oil
3 medium zucchini,
   trimmed and sliced
2 yellow bell peppers,
   deseeded and sliced
1 cup pine nuts
10 oz macaroni

12 oz cooked turkey
10-oz jar or can chargrilled
   artichokes, drained
   and sliced
3–4 plum tomatoes,
   quartered
4 tbsp freshly

   chopped cilantro
1 garlic clove, peeled
   and chopped
3 tbsp balsamic vinegar
salt and freshly ground
   black pepper

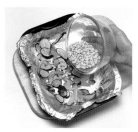

Preheat the oven to 400°F 15 minutes before cooking. Line a large roasting pan with foil, pour in half the olive oil, and place in the oven for 3 minutes, until hot. Remove from the oven, add the zucchini and bell peppers, and stir until evenly coated. Bake for 30–35 minutes, or until slightly charred, turning occasionally.

Add the pine nuts to the pan. Return to the oven and bake for 10 minutes, or until the pine nuts are toasted. Remove from the oven and let the vegetables cool completely.

Bring a large saucepan of lightly salted water to a boil. Add the macaroni and cook according to the package instructions, or until cooked but firm. Drain and refresh under cold running water, then drain thoroughly and place in a large salad bowl.

Cut the turkey into bite-sized pieces and add to the macaroni. Add the artichokes and tomatoes to the cooled vegetables and their juices in the pan. Blend together the cilantro, garlic, remaining oil, vinegar, and seasoning. Pour over the salad, toss lightly, and serve.

Hot Duck Pasta Salad

SERVES 6

3 boneless and skinless
    duck breasts
1 tbsp whole-grain mustard
1 tbsp clear honey
salt and freshly ground
    black pepper
4 medium eggs

1 lb fusilli pasta
1 cup green beans, trimmed
1 large carrot, peeled and
    cut into thin matchsticks
⅔ cup corn kernels, cooked
    if frozen
3 cups fresh baby spinach

leaves, shredded

For the dressing:
8 tbsp French dressing
1 tsp horseradish sauce
4 tbsp crème fraîche or
    sour cream

Preheat the oven to 400°F. Place the duck breasts on a baking sheet lined with foil. Mix together the whole-grain mustard and honey, season lightly with salt and pepper, then spread over the duck breasts. Roast in the preheated oven for 20–30 minutes, or until tender. Remove from the oven and keep warm.

Meanwhile, place the eggs in a small saucepan, cover with water, and bring to a boil. Simmer for 8 minutes, then drain. Bring a large saucepan of lightly salted water to a boil. Add the beans and pasta, return to a boil, and cook according to the package instructions for the pasta, or until cooked but firm. Drain the pasta and beans and refresh under cold running water.

Place the pasta and beans in a bowl, add the carrot, corn kernels, and spinach leaves, and toss lightly. Shell the eggs, cut into wedges, and arrange on top of the pasta. Slice the duck breasts, then place them on top of the salad. Beat the dressing ingredients together in a bowl until well blended, then drizzle over the salad. Serve immediately.

Try this: FOR AN ALTERNATIVE: 210 FOR KIDS: 234

Brown Rice & Lentil Salad with Duck

SERVES 6

1¼ cups lentils, rinsed
4 tbsp olive oil
1 medium onion, peeled and finely chopped
1¼ cups long-grain brown rice
½ tsp dried thyme
2 cups chicken stock
salt and freshly ground black pepper
12 oz shiitake or portobello mushrooms, trimmed and sliced

13 oz cooked Chinese-style spicy duck or roasted duck, sliced into chunks
2 garlic cloves, peeled and finely chopped
4 oz cooked smoked ham, diced
2 small zucchini, trimmed, diced, and blanched
6 green onions, trimmed and thinly sliced
2 tbsp freshly chopped parsley

2 tbsp walnut halves, toasted and chopped

For the dressing:
2 tbsp red or white wine vinegar
1 tbsp balsamic vinegar
1 tsp Dijon mustard
1 tsp clear honey
⅓ cup extra virgin olive oil
2–3 tbsp walnut oil

Bring a large saucepan of water to a boil, sprinkle in the lentils, return to a boil, then simmer over a low heat for 30 minutes, or until tender; do not overcook. Drain and rinse under cold running water, then drain again and reserve. Heat 2 tablespoons of the oil in a saucepan. Add the onion and cook for 2 minutes, until it begins to soften. Stir in the rice with the thyme and stock. Season to taste with salt and pepper and bring to a boil. Cover and simmer for 40 minutes, or until tender and the liquid is absorbed.

Heat the remaining oil in a large skillet and add the mushrooms. Cook for 5 minutes, until golden. Stir in the duck and garlic and cook for 2–3 minutes to heat through. Season well. To make the dressing, whisk the vinegars, mustard, and honey in a large serving bowl, then gradually whisk in the oils. Add the lentils and the rice, then stir lightly together. Gently stir in the ham, blanched zucchini, green onions, and parsley. Season to taste and sprinkle with the walnuts. Serve topped with the duck and mushrooms.

Try this: FOR AN ALTERNATIVE: 342 FOR KIDS: 378

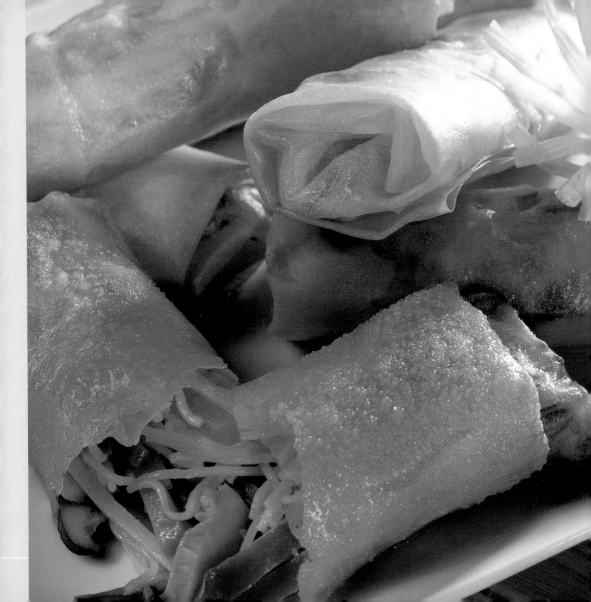

Appetizers: Vegetables & Salads

French Onion Tart

SERVES 4

For the quick,
    flaky pie shell:
½ cup (1 stick) butter
1½ cups all-purpose flour
pinch of salt

For the filling:
2 tbsp olive oil
4 large onions, peeled and
    thinly sliced
3 tbsp white wine vinegar
2 tbsp dark brown sugar

1½ cups Cheddar
    cheese, grated
a little beaten egg or milk
salt and freshly ground
    black pepper

Preheat the oven to 400°F. Place the butter in the freezer for 30 minutes. Sift the flour and salt into a large bowl. Remove the butter from the freezer and grate, using the coarse side of a grater – dip the butter in the flour every now and again to make it easier to grate. Mix the butter into the flour, using a knife, making sure all the butter is coated thoroughly with flour. Add 2 tablespoons of cold water and continue to mix, bringing the mixture together. Use your hands to complete the mixing. Add a little more water if needed to leave a clean bowl. Place the pastry in a plastic bag and chill in the refrigerator for 30 minutes.

Heat the oil in a large skillet, then fry the onions for 10 minutes, stirring occasionally until softened. Stir in the white wine vinegar and sugar. Increase the heat and stir frequently, for another 4–5 minutes, until the onions turn a deep caramel color. Cook for another 5 minutes, then reserve to cool.

On a lightly floured surface, roll out the dough to a 14-inch circle. Wrap over a rolling pin and move the circle on to a baking sheet. Sprinkle half the cheese over the pastry, leaving a 2-inch border around the edge, then spoon the caramelized onions over the cheese. Fold the uncovered dough edges over the edge of the filling to form a rim and brush the rim with beaten egg or milk. Season to taste with salt and pepper. Sprinkle over the remaining cheese and bake for 20–25 minutes. Transfer to a large plate and serve immediately.

Try this: FOR AN ALTERNATIVE: 248   FOR KIDS: 108

Red Pepper & Basil Tart

SERVES 4-6

For the olive pie shell:
2 cups all-purpose flour
pinch of salt
10 large black olives, pitted
    and finely chopped
1 medium egg, lightly
    beaten, plus 1 egg yolk
3 tbsp olive oil

For the filling:
2 large red bell peppers,
    quartered and deseeded
1½ cups mascarpone cheese
4 tbsp milk
2 medium eggs
3 tbsp freshly chopped basil
salt and freshly ground

black pepper
sprig of fresh basil,
    to garnish
mixed salad, to serve

Preheat the oven to 400°F 15 minutes before cooking. Sift the flour and salt into a bowl. Make a well in the center. Stir together the egg, oil, and 1 tablespoon of tepid water. Add to the dry ingredients, drop in the olives, and mix to make a dough. Knead on a lightly floured surface for a few seconds until smooth, then wrap in plastic wrap and chill in the refrigerator for 30 minutes.

Roll out the dough and use to line a 9-inch, loose-bottomed, fluted tart pan. Lightly prick the bottom with a fork. Cover and chill in the refrigerator for 20 minutes. Cook the bell peppers under a hot broiler for 10 minutes, or until the skins are blackened and blistered. Put the peppers in a plastic bag, cool for 10 minutes, then remove the skins and slice.

Line the pie shell with foil or greaseproof paper, weigh down with dry beans, and bake in the preheated oven for 10 minutes. Remove the foil and beans and bake for a further 5 minutes. Reduce the oven temperature to 350°F. Beat the mascarpone cheese until smooth. Gradually add the milk and eggs. Stir in the peppers and basil, and season to taste with salt and pepper. Spoon into the pie shell and bake for 25–30 minutes, or until lightly set. Garnish with a sprig of fresh basil and serve immediately with a mixed salad.

Try this: FOR AN ALTERNATIVE: 40 FOR KIDS: 264

Tomato & Zucchini Herb Tart

SERVES 4

4 tbsp olive oil
1 onion, peeled and
    finely chopped
3 garlic cloves, peeled
    and crushed
quick flaky pie shell (see

page 242), chilled
1 small egg, beaten
2 tbsp each freshly
    chopped rosemary
    and parsley
1½ cups rindless, fresh

soft goats' cheese
4 ripe plum tomatoes, sliced
1 medium zucchini, trimmed
    and sliced
thyme sprigs, to garnish

Preheat the oven to 450°F. Heat 2 tablespoons of the oil in a large skillet. Fry the onion and garlic for about 4 minutes until softened, and reserve.

Place the dough for the pie shell on a lightly floured surface and flatten it with a rolling pin to a 12-inch circle. Brush the dough with a little beaten egg, then prick all over with a fork.

Transfer onto a dampened baking sheet and bake in the preheated oven for 10 minutes. Turn the dough over and brush with a little more egg. Bake for 5 more minutes, then remove from the oven.

Mix together the onion, garlic, and herbs with the goats' cheese and spread over the dough. Arrange the tomatoes and zucchini over the goats' cheese and drizzle with the remaining oil.

Bake for 20–25 minutes, or until the pie shell is golden brown and the topping is bubbling. Garnish with the thyme sprigs and serve immediately.

Try this: FOR AN ALTERNATIVE: 356   FOR KIDS: 364

Leek & Potato Tart

SERVES 6

2 cups all-purpose flour
pinch of salt
½ cup (1 stick) plus
  2 tbsp butter, cubed
⅓ cup walnuts,
  finely chopped
1 large egg yolk

For the filling:
2 large leeks (about 1 lb),
  trimmed and thinly sliced
3 tbsp butter
3 medium potatoes (about
  1 lb), scrubbed
1¼ cups sour cream
3 medium eggs,

  lightly beaten
1½ cups Gruyère
  cheese, grated
freshly grated nutmeg
salt and freshly ground
  black pepper
fresh chives, to garnish

Preheat the oven to 400°F about 15 minutes before baking. Sift the flour and salt into a bowl. Rub in the butter until the mixture resembles bread crumbs. Stir in the nuts. Mix together the egg yolk and 3 tablespoons of cold water. Sprinkle over the dry ingredients. Mix to form a dough. Knead on a lightly floured surface for a few seconds, then wrap in plastic wrap and chill in the refrigerator for 20 minutes. Roll out and use to line an 8-inch spring-form pan or deep tart pan. Chill for a further 30 minutes.

Cook the leeks in the butter over a high heat for 2–3 minutes, stirring constantly. Lower the heat, cover, and cook for 25 minutes, until soft, stirring occasionally. Remove the leeks from the heat. Cook the potatoes in boiling salted water for 15 minutes, or until almost tender. Drain and thickly slice. Add to the leeks. Stir the sour cream into the leeks and potatoes, followed by the eggs, cheese, nutmeg, and salt and pepper. Pour into the pie shell and bake on the middle shelf in the preheated oven for 20 minutes.

Reduce the oven temperature to 375°F and cook for a further 30–35 minutes, or until the filling is set. Garnish with chives and serve immediately.

Try this: FOR AN ALTERNATIVE: 24 FOR KIDS: 266

Potato & Goats' Cheese Tart

SERVES 6

quick flaky pie shell
(see page 242), chilled
10 small waxy potatoes
(about 1¼ lb)
salt and freshly ground
black pepper
beaten egg, for brushing

2 tbsp sundried
tomato paste
¼ tsp chile powder,
or to taste
1 large egg
⅔ cup sour cream
⅔ cup milk

2 tbsp freshly
snipped chives
2¾ cups goats'
cheese, sliced
salad and warm crusty
bread, to serve

Preheat the oven to 375°F about 10 minutes before cooking. Roll out the dough for the quick flaky pie shell and line a 9-inch fluted tart pan. Chill in the refrigerator for 30 minutes.

Scrub the potatoes, place in a large saucepan of lightly salted water, and bring to a boil. Simmer for 10–15 minutes, or until the potatoes are tender. Drain and reserve until cool enough to handle.

Line the pie shell with greaseproof paper, weigh down with dried beans, and bake in the preheated oven for 15 minutes. Remove from the oven and discard the paper and beans. Brush the bottom with a little beaten egg, then return to the oven and cook for a further 5 minutes. Remove from the oven.

Cut the potatoes into ½-inch thick slices; reserve. Spread the sundried tomato paste over the pie shell, sprinkle with the chile powder, then arrange the potato slices on top in a decorative pattern. Beat together the egg, sour cream, milk, and chives, then season to taste with salt and pepper. Pour over the potatoes. Arrange the goats' cheese on top of the potatoes. Bake in the preheated oven for 30 minutes, until golden brown and set. Serve immediately with salad and warm crusty bread.

Try this: FOR AN ALTERNATIVE: 364 FOR KIDS: 242

Olive & Feta Parcels

MAKES 30

1 small red bell pepper
1 small yellow bell pepper
25–30 assorted marinated
   green and black olives

1 cup feta cheese
2 tbsp pine nuts,
   lightly toasted
6 sheets phyllo dough

3 tbsp olive oil
sour cream and chive
   dip, to serve

Preheat the broiler, then line the broiler rack with foil. Cut the peppers into quarters and remove the seeds. Place skin-side up on the foil-lined broiler rack and cook under the preheated broiler for 10 minutes, turning occasionally until the skins begin to blacken.

Preheat the oven to 350°F. Place the peppers in a plastic bag and let stand until cool enough to handle, then skin and thinly slice. Chop the olives and cut the feta cheese into small cubes. Mix together the olives, feta, sliced bell peppers, and pine nuts.

Cut one piece of phyllo dough in half, then brush with a little of the oil. Place a spoonful of the olive and feta mix about one-third of the way up the dough. Fold over the dough and wrap to form a square parcel that encases the filling completely.

Place this parcel in the center of the second half of the phyllo dough. Brush the edges lightly with a little oil, bring up the corners to meet in the center, and twist them loosely to form a purse. Brush with a little more oil and repeat with the remaining phyllo dough and filling.

Place the parcels on a lightly oiled baking sheet and bake in the preheated oven for 10–15 minutes, or until crisp and golden brown. Serve with the dip.

Try this: FOR AN ALTERNATIVE: 256 FOR KIDS: 124

Tortellini & Summer Vegetable Salad

SERVES 6

12 oz mixed green and plain cheese-filled fresh tortellini
⅔ cup extra virgin olive oil
2 cups fine green beans, trimmed
1 medium broccoli, cut into florets
1 yellow or red bell pepper, deseeded and thinly sliced
1 red onion, peeled and sliced
6-oz jar marinated artichoke hearts, drained and halved
2 tbsp capers
15 dry-cured pitted black olives
3 tbsp raspberry or balsamic vinegar
1 tbsp Dijon mustard
1 tsp brown sugar
salt and freshly ground black pepper
2 tbsp freshly chopped basil or flat-leaf parsley
2 hard-boiled eggs, quartered, to garnish

Bring a large saucepan of lightly salted water to a boil. Add the tortellini and cook according to the package instructions, or until cooked but firm. Using a large slatted spoon, transfer the tortellini to a colander to drain. Rinse under cold running water and drain again. Transfer to a large bowl and toss with 2 tablespoons of the olive oil.

Return the pasta water to a boil and drop in the green beans and broccoli florets; blanch them for 2 minutes, or until just beginning to soften. Drain, rinse under cold running water, and drain again thoroughly. Add the vegetables to the reserved tortellini. Add the pepper, onion, artichoke hearts, capers, and olives to the bowl; stir lightly.

Whisk together the vinegar, mustard, and brown sugar in a bowl, and season to taste with salt and pepper. Slowly whisk in the remaining olive oil to form a thick, creamy dressing. Pour over the tortellini and vegetables, add the chopped basil or parsley, and stir until lightly coated. Transfer to a shallow serving dish or salad bowl. Garnish with the hard-boiled egg quarters and serve.

Try this: FOR AN ALTERNATIVE: 296   FOR KIDS: 162

Mozzarella Parcels with Cranberry Relish

SERVES 6

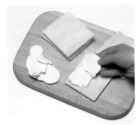

1 cup mozzarella cheese
8 slices of thin white bread
2 medium eggs, beaten
salt and freshly ground
    black pepper

1¼ cups olive oil

For the relish:
1 cup cranberries
2 tbsp fresh orange juice

grated rind of
    1 small orange
¼ cup light brown sugar
1 tbsp port

Slice the mozzarella thinly, remove the crusts from the bread, and make sandwiches with the bread and cheese. Cut into 2-inch squares and squash them flat. Season the eggs with salt and pepper, then soak the bread in the seasoned egg for 1 minute on each side, until well coated.

Heat the oil to 375°F and deep-fry the bread squares for 1–2 minutes, or until they are crisp and golden brown. Drain on a paper towel and keep warm while the cranberry relish is being prepared.

Place the cranberries, orange juice, rind, sugar, and port into a small saucepan and add 5 tablespoons of water. Bring to a boil, then simmer for 10 minutes, or until the cranberries 'pop'. Sweeten with a little more sugar if necessary.

Arrange the mozzarella parcels on individual serving plates. Serve with a little of the cranberry relish.

Try this: FOR AN ALTERNATIVE: 176   FOR KIDS: 164

Bruschetta with Pecorino, Garlic, & Tomatoes

SERVES 4

6 ripe but firm tomatoes
½ cup pecorino cheese,
   finely grated
1 tbsp oregano leaves
salt and freshly ground

black pepper
3 tbsp olive oil
3 garlic cloves, peeled
8 slices of flat Italian bread,
   such as focaccia

½ cup mozzarella cheese
marinated black olives,
   to serve

Preheat the broiler and line the broiler rack with foil just before cooking. Make a small cross in the top of the tomatoes, then place in a small bowl and cover with boiling water. Let stand for 2 minutes, then drain and remove the skins. Cut into quarters, remove the seeds, and chop the flesh into small cubes.

Mix the tomato flesh with the pecorino cheese and 2 teaspoons of the fresh oregano, and season to taste with salt and pepper. Add 1 tablespoon of the olive oil and mix thoroughly.

Crush the garlic and spread evenly over the slices of bread. Heat 2 tablespoons of the olive oil in a large skillet and fry the bread slices until they are crisp and golden.

Place the fried bread on a lightly oiled baking sheet and spoon on the tomato and cheese topping. Place a little mozzarella on top and place under the preheated broiler for 3–4 minutes, until golden and bubbling. Garnish with the remaining oregano, then arrange the bruschettas on a serving plate and serve immediately with the olives.

Try this: FOR AN ALTERNATIVE: 206   FOR KIDS: 256

Sweet Potato Cakes with Mango & Tomato Salsa

SERVES 4

3 large sweet potatoes
(about 1½ lb), peeled and
cut into large chunks
salt and freshly ground
black pepper
2 tbsp butter
1 onion, peeled
and chopped
1 garlic clove, peeled
and crushed

pinch of freshly
grated nutmeg
1 medium egg, beaten
⅓ cup quick-cook polenta
2 tbsp sunflower oil

For the salsa:
1 ripe mango, peeled,
stoned, and diced
6 cherry tomatoes,

cut in wedges
4 green onions, trimmed
and thinly sliced
1 red chile pepper, deseeded
and finely chopped
finely grated rind and juice
of ½ lime
2 tbsp freshly chopped mint
1 tsp clear honey
lettuce leaves, to serve

Steam or cook the sweet potatoes in lightly salted boiling water for 15–20 minutes, until tender. Drain well, then mash until smooth.

Melt the butter in a saucepan. Add the onion and garlic, and cook gently for 10 minutes, until soft. Add to the mashed sweet potato and season with the nutmeg, salt, and pepper. Stir together until mixed thoroughly. Let cool.

Shape the mixture into four oval potato cakes, about 1 inch thick. Dip first in the beaten egg, allowing the excess to fall back into the bowl, then coat in the polenta. Refrigerate for at least 30 minutes.

Meanwhile, mix together all the ingredients for the salsa. Spoon into a serving bowl, cover with plastic wrap, and let stand at room temperature to allow the flavors to develop.

Heat the oil in a skillet and cook the potato cakes for 4–5 minutes on each side. Serve with the salsa and lettuce leaves.

Try this: FOR AN ALTERNATIVE: 128   FOR KIDS: 372

Stuffed Tomatoes with Broiled Polenta

SERVES 4

For the polenta:
1¼ cups vegetable stock
salt and freshly ground
    black pepper
⅓ cup quick-cook polenta
1 tbsp butter

For the stuffed tomatoes:
4 large tomatoes
1 tbsp olive oil
1 garlic clove, peeled
    and crushed
1 bunch green onions,
    trimmed and
    finely chopped

2 tbsp freshly
    chopped parsley
2 tbsp freshly chopped basil
2 slices Parma ham or
    prosciutto, cut into slivers
1 cup fresh white
    bread crumbs
snipped chives, to garnish

Preheat the broiler just before cooking. To make the polenta, pour the stock into a saucepan. Add a pinch of salt and bring to a boil. Pour in the polenta in a fine stream, stirring all the time. Simmer for about 15 minutes, or until thick. Stir in the butter and add a little pepper. Turn the polenta out onto a cutting board and spread to a thickness of just over ½ inch. Cool, cover with plastic wrap, and chill in the refrigerator for 30 minutes.

To make the stuffed tomatoes, cut the tomatoes in half, then scoop out the seeds and press through a fine sieve to extract the juices. Reserve the juices. Season the insides of the tomatoes with salt and pepper and reserve. Heat the olive oil in a saucepan and gently fry the garlic and green onions for 3 minutes. Add the tomatoes' juices and let boil for 3–4 minutes, until most of the liquid has evaporated. Stir in the herbs, Parma ham, and a little black pepper with half the bread crumbs. Spoon into the hollowed out tomatoes and reserve.

Cut the polenta into 2-inch squares, then cut each in half diagonally to make triangles. Put the triangles on a piece of foil and broil for 4–5 minutes on each side, until golden. Keep warm. Broil the tomatoes under a medium broiler for 4 minutes – any exposed Parma ham will become crisp. Sprinkle with the remaining bread crumbs and broil for 1–2 minutes, or until the bread crumbs are golden brown. Garnish with snipped chives and serve immediately with the broiled polenta.

Vegetable Frittata

SERVES 2

6 medium eggs
2 tbsp freshly
    chopped parsley
1 tbsp freshly
    chopped tarragon
4 tbsp finely grated pecorino
    or Parmesan cheese
freshly ground black pepper

4–5 small new potatoes
    (about 6 oz)
2 small carrots, peeled
    and sliced
1 small broccoli, cut
    into florets
1 zucchini, sliced
2 tbsp olive oil

4 green onions, trimmed
    and thinly sliced

To serve:
mixed green salad
crusty Italian bread

Preheat the broiler just before cooking. Lightly beat the eggs with the parsley, tarragon, and half the cheese. Season to taste with black pepper and reserve – salt is not needed because the pecorino is salty.

Bring a large saucepan of lightly salted water to a boil. Add the new potatoes and cook for 8 minutes. Add the carrots and cook for 4 minutes, then add the broccoli florets and the zucchini and cook for a further 3–4 minutes, or until all the vegetables are just tender. Drain well.

Heat the oil in an 8-inch heavy-based skillet. Add the green onions and cook for 3–4 minutes, or until softened. Add all the vegetables and cook for a few seconds, then pour in the beaten egg mixture. Stir gently for about a minute, then cook for a further 1–2 minutes, or until the bottom of the frittata is set and golden brown.

Place the skillet under a hot broiler for 1 minute, or until almost set and just beginning to brown. Sprinkle with the remaining cheese and broil for a further 1 minute, or until it is lightly browned. Loosen the edges and slide out of the pan. Cut into wedges and serve hot or warm with a mixed green salad and crusty Italian bread.

Try this: FOR AN ALTERNATIVE: 304   FOR KIDS: 190

Mediterranean Potato Salad

SERVES 4

14–16 small waxy potatoes
  (about 1½ lb)
2 red onions, peeled and
  roughly chopped
1 yellow and green bell
  pepper each, deseeded
  and roughly chopped
6 tbsp extra virgin olive oil

1 medium tomato, chopped
10 pitted black olives, sliced
1 cup feta cheese
3 tbsp freshly
  chopped parsley
2 tbsp white wine vinegar
1 tsp Dijon mustard
1 tsp clear honey

salt and freshly ground
  black pepper
sprigs of fresh parsley,
  to garnish

Preheat the oven to 400°F. Place the potatoes in a large saucepan of salted water, bring to a boil, and simmer until just tender. Do not overcook. Drain and plunge into cold water to stop the potatoes from cooking further.

Place the onions in a bowl with the yellow and green peppers, then pour over 2 tablespoons of the olive oil. Stir and spoon onto a large baking sheet. Cook in the preheated oven for 25–30 minutes, or until the vegetables are tender and lightly charred in places, turning them occasionally. Remove from the oven and transfer to a large bowl.

Cut the potatoes into bite-sized pieces and mix with the roasted onions and peppers. Add the tomatoes and olives to the potatoes. Crumble over the feta cheese and sprinkle with the chopped parsley.

Whisk together the remaining olive oil, vinegar, mustard, and honey, then season to taste with salt and pepper. Pour the dressing over the potatoes and toss gently together. Garnish with parsley sprigs and serve immediately.

Try this: FOR AN ALTERNATIVE: 150   FOR KIDS: 102

Pasta Triangles with Pesto & Walnut Dressing

SERVES 6

1 lb fresh egg lasagne
4 tbsp ricotta cheese
4 tbsp pesto
1 cup shelled walnuts
1 slice white bread,
   crusts removed
⅔ cup sour cream

¾ cup mascarpone cheese
2 tbsp pecorino
   cheese, grated
salt and freshly ground
   black pepper
1 tbsp olive oil
sprig of dill or freshly

chopped basil or parsley,
   to garnish
tomato and cucumber salad,
   to serve

Preheat the broiler to high. Cut the lasagne pieces in half, then into triangles, and reserve. Mix the pesto and ricotta cheese together and warm gently in a pan.

Toast the walnuts under the preheated broiler until golden. Rub off the papery skins. Place the nuts in a food processor with the bread and grind finely. Mix the sour cream with the mascarpone cheese in a bowl. Add the ground walnuts and grated pecorino cheese and season to taste with salt and pepper. Whisk in the olive oil. Pour into a pan and warm gently.

Bring a large saucepan of lightly salted water to a boil. Add the pasta triangles and cook, according to the package instructions, about 3–4 minutes, or until cooked but firm.

Drain the pasta thoroughly and arrange a few triangles on each serving plate. Top each one with a spoonful of the pesto mixture then place another triangle on top. Continue to layer the pasta and pesto mixture, then spoon a little of the walnut sauce on top of each stack. Garnish with dill, basil, or parsley, and serve immediately with a freshly dressed tomato and cucumber salad.

Try this: FOR AN ALTERNATIVE: 230 FOR KIDS: 228

Pastini-stuffed Peppers

SERVES 6

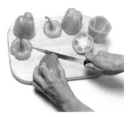

6 red, yellow, or orange bell peppers, tops cut off and deseeded
salt and freshly ground black pepper
6 oz pastini
4 tbsp olive oil
1 onion, peeled and finely chopped
2 garlic cloves, peeled and finely chopped
3 ripe plum tomatoes, skinned, deseeded, and chopped
¼ cup dry white wine
8 pitted black olives, chopped
4 tbsp freshly chopped mixed herbs, such as parsley, basil, oregano, or marjoram
1 cup mozzarella cheese, diced
4 tbsp grated Parmesan cheese
fresh tomato sauce, preferably homemade, to serve

Preheat the oven to 375°F 10 minutes before cooking. Bring a saucepan of water to a boil. Trim the bottom of each pepper so it sits straight. Blanch the peppers for 2–3 minutes, then drain on a paper towel. Return the water to a boil, add a pinch of salt and the pastini, and cook for 3–4 minutes, or until cooked but firm. Drain thoroughly. Rinse under cold running water, drain again, and reserve.

Heat 2 tablespoons of the olive oil in a large skillet, add the onion, and cook for 3–4 minutes. Add the garlic and cook for 1 minute. Stir in the tomatoes and wine and cook for 5 minutes, stirring frequently. Add the olives, herbs, mozzarella cheese, and half the Parmesan cheese. Season to taste with salt and pepper. Remove from the heat and stir in the pastini.

Dry the insides of the peppers with a paper towel, then season lightly. Arrange the peppers in a lightly oiled shallow baking dish and fill with the pastini mixture. Sprinkle with the remaining Parmesan cheese and drizzle over the remaining oil. Pour in boiling water to come ½ inch up the sides of the dish. Cook in the preheated oven for 25 minutes, or until cooked. Serve immediately with freshly made tomato sauce.

Try this: FOR AN ALTERNATIVE: 278   FOR KIDS: 366

Rigatoni with Roasted
Beet & Arugula

SERVES 4

7 raw beets (about 12 oz),
   unpeeled
1 garlic clove, peeled
   and crushed
½ tsp finely grated

orange rind
1 tbsp orange juice
1 tsp lemon juice
2 tbsp walnut oil
salt and black pepper

12 oz dried rigatoni
3 cups arugula
1 cup Dolcelatte or
   Gorgonzola cheese,
   cut into small cubes

Preheat the oven to 300°F 10 minutes before cooking. Wrap the beets individually in foil and bake for 1–1½ hours, or until tender. Test them by opening one of the parcels and scraping the skin away from the stem end – it should come off easily.

Let the beets cool enough to handle, then peel and cut each beet into six to eight wedges, depending on the size. Mix the garlic, orange rind and juice, lemon juice, walnut oil, and salt and pepper together, then drizzle over the beets and toss to coat well.

Meanwhile, bring a large saucepan of lightly salted water to a boil. Cook the pasta for 10 minutes, or until cooked but firm.

Drain the pasta thoroughly, then add the warm beets, arugula, and Dolcelatte or Gorgonzola cheese. Quickly and gently toss together, then divide between serving bowls and serve immediately before the arugula wilts.

Try this: FOR AN ALTERNATIVE: 306   FOR KIDS: 224

Peperonata

SERVES 6

2 red bell peppers
2 yellow bell peppers
3 medium waxy potatoes
   (about 1 lb)
1 large onion
2 tbsp virgin olive oil

5–6 medium tomatoes
   (about 1½ lb), peeled,
   deseeded, and chopped
2 small zucchini
10 pitted black olives,
   quartered

small handful basil leaves
salt and freshly ground
   black pepper
crusty bread, to serve

Prepare the bell peppers by halving them lengthwise and removing the stems, seeds, and membranes. Cut the peppers lengthwise into strips about ½ inch wide. Peel the potatoes and roughly dice them, about 1–1¼ inches across. Cut the onion lengthwise into eight wedges.

Heat the olive oil in a large saucepan over a medium heat. Add the onion and cook for about 5 minutes, or until starting to brown.

Add the peppers, potatoes, tomatoes, zucchini, black olives, and about four torn basil leaves. Season to taste with salt and pepper.

Stir the mixture, cover, and cook over a low heat for about 40 minutes, or until the vegetables are tender but still hold their shape. Garnish with the remaining basil. Transfer to a serving bowl and serve immediately, with chunks of crusty bread.

Try this: FOR AN ALTERNATIVE: 270   FOR KIDS: 330

Layered Cheese & Herb Potato Cake

SERVES 4

6 medium waxy potatoes
(about 2 lb)
3 tbsp freshly
snipped chives
2 tbsp freshly
chopped parsley
2 cups mature

Cheddar cheese
2 large egg yolks
1 tsp paprika
2½ cups fresh white
bread crumbs
½ cup almonds, toasted and
roughly chopped

4 tbsp butter, melted
salt and freshly ground
black pepper
mixed salad or steamed
vegetables, to serve

Preheat the oven to 350°F. Lightly oil and line the bottom of an 8-inch round cake pan with lightly oiled greaseproof paper or baking parchment. Peel and thinly slice the potatoes and reserve. Stir the chives, parsley, cheese, and egg yolks together in a small bowl and reserve. Mix the paprika into the bread crumbs.

Sprinkle the almonds over the bottom of the lined pan. Cover with half the potatoes, arranging them in layers, then sprinkle with the paprika-bread crumb mixture and season to taste with salt and pepper.

Spoon the cheese and herb mixture over the bread crumbs, along with a little more seasoning, then arrange the remaining potatoes on top. Drizzle over the melted butter and press the surface down firmly.

Bake in the preheated oven for 1¼ hours, or until golden and cooked through. Let the pan stand for 10 minutes before carefully turning out and cutting into thick wedges. Serve immediately with salad or freshly cooked vegetables.

Try this: FOR AN ALTERNATIVE: 248   FOR KIDS: 132

Italian Baked Tomatoes with Curly Endive & Radicchio

SERVES 4

1 tsp olive oil
4 beef tomatoes
salt
1 cup fresh white
   bread crumbs
1 tbsp freshly
   snipped chives
1 tbsp freshly

chopped parsley
1½ cup mushrooms,
   finely chopped
salt and freshly ground
   black pepper
2 tbsp fresh Parmesan
   cheese, grated

For the salad:
½ head curly endive
½ small piece of radicchio
2 tbsp olive oil
1 tsp balsamic vinegar
salt and freshly ground
   black pepper

Preheat the oven to 375°F. Lightly oil a baking sheet with the teaspoon of oil. Slice the tops off the tomatoes, remove all the tomato flesh, and sieve into a large bowl. Sprinkle a little salt inside the tomato shells and place them upside down on a plate while the filling is prepared.

Mix the sieved tomato with the bread crumbs, fresh herbs, and mushrooms, and season well with salt and pepper. Place the tomato shells on the prepared baking sheet and fill with the tomato and mushroom mixture. Sprinkle the cheese on top and bake in the preheated oven for 15–20 minutes, until golden brown.

Meanwhile, prepare the salad. Arrange the endive and radicchio on individual serving plates and mix the remaining ingredients together in a small bowl to make the dressing. Season to taste.

When the tomatoes are cooked, let rest for 5 minutes, then place on the prepared plates and drizzle over a little dressing. Serve warm.

Try this: FOR AN ALTERNATIVE: 262   FOR KIDS: 180

Mediterranean Rice Salad

SERVES 4

1⅓ cups brown rice
2 sundried tomatoes, finely chopped
2 garlic cloves, peeled and finely chopped
4 tbsp oil from a jar of sundried tomatoes
2 tsp balsamic vinegar
2 tsp red wine vinegar

salt and freshly ground black pepper
1 red onion, peeled and thinly sliced
1 yellow bell pepper, quartered and deseeded
1 red bell pepper, quartered and deseeded
½ cucumber, peeled

and diced
6 ripe plum tomatoes, cut into wedges
1 fennel bulb, halved and thinly sliced
fresh basil leaves, to garnish

Cook the rice in a saucepan of lightly salted boiling water for 35–40 minutes, or until tender. Drain well and reserve.

Whisk the sundried tomatoes, garlic, oil, and vinegars together in a small bowl or jug. Season to taste with salt and pepper. Put the red onion in a large bowl, pour over the dressing, and let stand to allow the flavors to develop.

Put the peppers, skin-side up, on a broiler rack and cook under a preheated hot broiler for 5–6 minutes, or until blackened and charred. Remove and place in a plastic bag. When cool enough to handle, peel off the skins and slice the peppers.

Add the peppers, cucumber, tomatoes, fennel, and rice to the onions. Mix gently together to coat in the dressing. Cover and chill in the refrigerator for 30 minutes to allow the flavors to mingle.

Remove the salad from the refrigerator and let stand at room temperature for 20 minutes. Garnish with fresh basil leaves and serve.

Try this: FOR AN ALTERNATIVE: 208   FOR KIDS: 210

Warm Potato, Pear, & Pecan Salad

SERVES 4

18–24 new potatoes
 (about 2 lb), preferably
 red-skinned, unpeeled
salt and freshly ground
 black pepper

1 tsp Dijon mustard
2 tsp white wine vinegar
3 tbsp peanut oil
1 tbsp hazelnut or walnut oil
2 tsp poppy seeds

2 firm, ripe pears
2 tsp lemon juice
6 cups spinach leaves
 (about 6 oz)
¾ cup toasted pecans

Scrub the potatoes, then cook in a saucepan of lightly salted boiling water for 15 minutes, or until tender. Drain, cut into halves, or quarters if large, and place in a serving bowl.

In a small bowl or jug, whisk together the mustard and vinegar. Gradually add the oils until the mixture begins to thicken. Stir in the poppy seeds and season to taste with salt and pepper.

Pour about two-thirds of the dressing over the hot potatoes and toss gently to coat. Let stand until the potatoes have soaked up the dressing and are just warm.

Meanwhile, quarter and core the pears. Cut into thin slices, then sprinkle with the lemon juice to prevent them from turning brown. Add to the potatoes with the spinach leaves and toasted pecans. Gently mix together. Drizzle the remaining dressing over the salad. Serve immediately before the spinach starts to wilt.

Try this: FOR AN ALTERNATIVE: 226 FOR KIDS: 234

Wild Garlic Mushrooms with Pizza Breadsticks

SERVES 6

For the breadsticks:
1 tbsp dried yeast
1 cup warm water
3½ cups all-purpose flour
2–3 tbsp olive oil
1 red bell pepper, deseeded
2 oz grated cheddar cheese
1 tsp salt

For the mushrooms:
6 tbsp olive oil
4 garlic cloves, peeled
    and crushed
6½ cups mixed wild
    mushrooms (about 1 lb),
    cleaned and dried
salt and freshly ground

black pepper
1 tbsp freshly
    chopped parsley
1 tbsp freshly chopped basil
1 tsp fresh oregano leaves
2 tbsp lemon juice

Preheat the oven to 475°F 15 minutes before baking. Place the dried yeast in the warm water for 10 minutes. Place the flour in a large bowl and gradually blend in 1 tablespoon of the olive oil, the salt, and the dissolved yeast.

Knead on a lightly floured surface to form a smooth and pliable dough. Cover with plastic wrap and let stand in a warm place for 15 minutes to allow the dough to rise, then roll out again and cut into sticks of equal length. Cover and let rise again for 10 minutes. Brush with 1–2 tablespoons of olive oil. Cut the pepper into thin strips and arrange on top of the dough. Sprinkle over the cheese and then the salt, and bake in the preheated oven for 10 minutes.

Pour 2 tablespoons of the oil into a skillet and add the crushed garlic. Cook over a low heat, stirring well for 3–4 minutes to flavor the oil. Cut the wild mushrooms into bite-sized slices if large, then add to the pan. Season well with salt and pepper and cook gently for 6–8 minutes, or until tender.

Whisk the fresh herbs, remaining olive oil, and lemon juice together, then pour over the mushrooms and heat through. Season to taste and place on individual serving dishes. Serve with the pizza breadsticks.

Try this: FOR AN ALTERNATIVE: 312   FOR KIDS: 376

Vegetable Tempura

SERVES 4-6

1 cup rice flour
¾ cup all-purpose flour
4 tsp baking powder
1 tbsp dried
   mustard powder
2 tsp semolina
salt and freshly ground

black pepper
1¼ cups peanut oil
¾ medium zucchini, trimmed
   and thickly sliced
1½ cups snow peas
24 ears baby sweet corn
4 small red onions, peeled

and quartered
1 large red bell pepper,
   deseeded and cut into
   1-inch wide strips
light soy sauce, to serve

Sift the rice flour and all-purpose flour into a large bowl, then sift in the baking powder and dried mustard powder.

Stir the semolina into the flour mixture and season to taste with salt and pepper. Gradually beat in 1¼ cups of cold water to produce a thin coating batter. Let stand at room temperature for 30 minutes.

Heat a wok or large skillet, add the oil, and heat to 350°F. Working in batches, and using a slatted spoon, dip the vegetables in the batter until well coated, then drop them carefully into the hot oil. Cook each batch for 2–3 minutes, or until golden. Drain on a paper towel and keep warm while cooking the remaining batches.

Transfer the vegetables to a warmed serving platter and serve immediately with the light soy sauce to use as a dipping sauce.

Indonesian Salad with Peanut Dressing

SERVES 4

5–6 new potatoes (about 8 oz), scrubbed
1 large carrot, peeled and cut into matchsticks
1 cup green beans, trimmed
2 cups cauliflower florets
½ medium cucumber, cut into matchsticks
¾–1 cup fresh bean sprouts

3 medium eggs, hard-boiled and quartered

For the peanut dressing:
2 tbsp sesame oil
1 garlic clove, peeled and crushed
1 red chile pepper, deseeded and finely chopped

½ cup crunchy peanut butter
6 tbsp hot vegetable stock
2 tsp light brown sugar
2 tsp dark soy sauce
1 tbsp lime juice

Cook the potatoes in a saucepan of boiling salted water for 15–20 minutes, until tender. Remove with a slatted spoon and thickly slice into a large bowl. Keep the saucepan of water boiling.

Add the carrot, green beans, and cauliflower to the water, return to a boil, and cook for 2 minutes, or until just tender. Drain and refresh under cold running water, then drain well. Add to the potatoes with the cucumber and bean sprouts.

To make the dressing, gently heat the sesame oil in a small saucepan. Add the garlic and chile pepper and cook for a few seconds, then remove from the heat. Stir in the peanut butter.

Stir in the stock, a little at a time. Add the remaining ingredients and mix together to make a thick, creamy dressing.

Divide the vegetables between four plates and arrange the eggs on top. Drizzle the dressing over the salad and serve immediately.

Try this: FOR AN ALTERNATIVE: 338 FOR KIDS: 228

Spaghettini with Lemon Pesto & Cheese & Herb Bread

SERVES 4

1 small onion, peeled
and grated
2 tsp freshly
chopped oregano
1 tbsp freshly
chopped parsley
6 tbsp butter
½ cup pecorino or Parmesan

cheese, grated
8 slices of Italian flat bread
10 oz dried spaghettini
4 tbsp olive oil
1 large bunch of basil
½ cup pine nuts
1 garlic clove, peeled
and crushed

⅓ cup Parmesan
cheese, grated
finely grated rind and juice
of 2 lemons
salt and freshly ground
black pepper
4 tsp butter

Preheat the oven to 400°F 15 minutes before baking. Mix together the onion, oregano, parsley, butter, and pecorino cheese. Spread the bread with the cheese mixture, place on a lightly oiled baking sheet, and cover with foil. Bake in the preheated oven for 10–15 minutes, then keep warm.

Add the spaghettini with 1 tablespoon of olive oil to a large saucepan of fast-boiling, lightly salted water, and cook for 3–4 minutes, or until cooked but firm. Drain, reserving 2 tablespoons of the cooking liquid.

Blend the basil, pine nuts, garlic, Parmesan cheese, lemon rind and juice, and remaining olive oil in a food processor or blender until a puree is formed. Season to taste with salt and pepper, then place in a saucepan.

Heat the lemon pesto gently until piping hot, then stir in the pasta, together with the reserved cooking liquor. Add the butter and mix well together. Add plenty of black pepper to the pasta and serve immediately with the warm cheese and herb bread.

Try this: FOR AN ALTERNATIVE: 332 FOR KIDS: 374

Zucchini & Tarragon Tortilla

SERVES 6

4–5 medium potatoes (about 1½ lb)
3 tbsp olive oil
1 onion, peeled and thinly sliced
salt and black pepper
1 zucchini, trimmed and thinly sliced
6 medium eggs
2 tbsp freshly chopped tarragon
tomato wedges, to serve

Peel the potatoes and thinly slice. Dry the slices on a clean kitchen towel, getting them as dry as possible. Heat the oil in a large, heavy-based pan, add the onion, and cook for 3 minutes. Add the potatoes with a little salt and pepper, then stir the potatoes and onion lightly to coat in the oil.

Reduce the heat to the lowest setting, cover, and cook gently for 5 minutes. Turn the potatoes and onion over and continue to cook for a further 5 minutes. Give the pan a shake every now and again to ensure that the potatoes do not stick to the bottom or burn. Add the zucchini, then cover and cook for a further 10 minutes.

Beat the eggs and tarragon together and season to taste with salt and pepper. Pour the egg mixture over the vegetables and return to the heat. Cook on a low heat for up to 20–25 minutes, or until there is no liquid egg left on the surface of the tortilla.

Turn the tortilla over by inverting the tortilla onto the lid or a flat plate. Return the tortilla to the pan and the heat, and cook for a final 3–5 minutes, or until the underside is golden brown. Or, if you prefer, place the tortilla under a preheated broiler for 4 minutes, or until set and golden brown on top. Cut into slices and serve hot or cold with tomato wedges.

Try this: FOR AN ALTERNATIVE: 264   FOR KIDS: 190

Eggplant & Yogurt Dip

MAKES 1 pint

2 eggplants (about 16 oz)
1 tbsp light olive oil
1 tbsp lemon juice
2 garlic cloves, peeled
  and crushed
6¾-oz jar pimentos, drained

⅔ cup plain yogurt
salt and freshly ground
  black pepper
6 black olives, pitted and
  chopped
2 cups cauliflower florets

1 medium–large broccoli,
  cut into florets
1–2 medium carrots,
  peeled and cut into
  2-inch strips

Preheat the oven to 400°F. Pierce the skin of the eggplant with a fork and place on a baking sheet. Cook for 40 minutes or until soft.

Cool the eggplant, then cut in half, and scoop out the flesh and tip into a bowl. Mash the eggplant with the olive oil, lemon juice, and garlic until smooth, or blend for a few seconds in a food processor.

Chop the pimentos into small cubes and add to the eggplant mixture. When blended, add the yogurt. Stir well and season to taste with salt and pepper. Add the chopped olives and chill in the refrigerator for at least 30 minutes.

Place the cauliflower and broccoli florets and carrot strips into a saucepan and cover with boiling water. Simmer for 2 minutes, then rinse in cold water. Drain and serve as crudités to accompany the dip.

Try this: FOR AN ALTERNATIVE: 316   FOR KIDS: 310

Tortellini, Cherry Tomato, & Mozzarella Skewers

SERVES 6

9 oz mixed green and plain cheese or vegetable-filled fresh tortellini
⅔ cup extra virgin olive oil
2 garlic cloves, peeled and crushed

pinch dried thyme or basil
salt and freshly ground black pepper
12–14 cherry tomatoes
1 lb mozzarella, cut into 1-inch cubes

basil leaves, to garnish
dressed lettuce leaves, to serve

Preheat the broiler and line a broiler pan with foil just before cooking. Bring a large saucepan of lightly salted water to a boil. Add the tortellini to the saucepan and cook, according to the package instructions, or until cooked but firm. Drain, rinse under cold running water, drain again, and toss with 2 tablespoons of the olive oil and reserve.

Pour the remaining olive oil into a small bowl. Add the crushed garlic and thyme or basil, then blend well. Season to taste with salt and black pepper and reserve.

To assemble the skewers, thread the tortellini alternately with the cherry tomatoes and cubes of mozzarella. Arrange the skewers on the broiler pan and brush generously on all sides with the olive oil mixture.

Cook the skewers under the preheated broiler for about 5 minutes, or until they begin to turn golden, turning them halfway through cooking. Arrange two skewers on each plate and garnish with a few basil leaves. Serve immediately with dressed lettuce leaves.

Try this: FOR AN ALTERNATIVE: 216   FOR KIDS: 106

Mixed Canapés

SERVES 12

For the stir-fried
  cheese canapés:
6 thick slices white bread
3 tbsp butter, softened
¾ cup sharp Cheddar cheese,
  grated
¾ cup blue cheese,

such as Stilton or
  Gorgonzola, crumbled
3 tbsp sunflower oil

For the spicy nuts:
2 tbsp unsalted butter
2 tbsp light olive oil

1½ cups mixed
  unsalted nuts
1 tsp ground paprika
½ tsp ground cumin
½ tsp fine sea salt
sprigs of fresh cilantro,
  to garnish

For the cheese canapés, cut the crusts off the bread, then gently roll with a rolling pin to flatten slightly. Thinly spread with butter, then sprinkle over the mixed cheeses as evenly as possible.

Roll up each slice tightly, then cut into four sections, each about 1 inch long. Heat the oil in a wok or large skillet and stir-fry the cheese rolls in two batches, turning them all the time until golden brown and crisp. Drain on a paper towel and serve warm or cold.

For the spicy nuts, melt the butter and oil in a wok, then add the nuts and stir-fry over a low heat for about 5 minutes, stirring all the time, or until they begin to color. Sprinkle the paprika and cumin over the nuts and continue stir-frying for a further 1–2 minutes, or until the nuts are golden brown.

Remove from the wok and drain on a paper towel. Sprinkle with the salt, garnish with sprigs of fresh cilantro, and serve hot or cold. If serving cold, store both the cheese canapés and the spicy nuts in airtight containers.

Try this: FOR AN ALTERNATIVE: 104   FOR KIDS: 122

Mozzarella Frittata
with Tomato & Basil Salad

SERVES 6

For the salad:
6 firm, ripe tomatoes
2 tbsp fresh basil leaves
2 tbsp olive oil
1 tbsp fresh lemon juice
1 tsp superfine sugar

freshly ground black pepper

For the frittata:
7 medium eggs, beaten
salt
3 cups mozzarella cheese

(about 11 oz)
2 green onions, trimmed
and finely chopped
2 tbsp olive oil
warm crusty bread, to serve

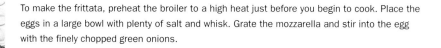

To make the tomato and basil salad, slice the tomatoes thinly, tear up the basil leaves, and sprinkle over. Make the dressing by whisking the olive oil, lemon juice, and sugar together well. Season with black pepper before drizzling the dressing over the salad.

To make the frittata, preheat the broiler to a high heat just before you begin to cook. Place the eggs in a large bowl with plenty of salt and whisk. Grate the mozzarella and stir into the egg with the finely chopped green onions.

Heat the oil in a large, nonstick skillet and pour in the egg mixture, stirring with a wooden spoon to spread the ingredients evenly over the pan.

Cook for 5–8 minutes, until the frittata is golden brown and firm on the underside. Place the whole pan under the preheated broiler and cook for about 4–5 minutes, or until the top is golden brown. Slide the frittata onto a serving plate, cut into six large wedges, and serve immediately with the tomato and basil salad and plenty of warm crusty bread.

Carrot, Celeriac, & Sesame Seed Salad

SERVES 6

1½ cups celeriac (about 8 oz)
3 medium carrots, peeled
5 tbsp seedless raisins
2 tbsp sesame seeds
freshly chopped parsley,
   to garnish

For the lemon &
   chile dressing:
grated rind of 1 lemon
4 tbsp lemon juice
2 tbsp sunflower oil
2 tbsp clear honey

1 red bird's eye chile
   pepper, deseeded
   and finely chopped
salt and freshly ground
   black pepper

Slice the celeriac into thin matchsticks. Place in a small saucepan of boiling salted water and boil for 2 minutes.

Drain and rinse the celeriac in cold water and place in a mixing bowl. Finely grate the carrots. Add the carrot and the raisins to the celeriac in the bowl.

Place the sesame seeds under a hot broiler or dry-fry in a skillet for 1–2 minutes, until golden brown, then let cool.

Make the dressing by whisking together the lemon rind, lemon juice, oil, honey, chile pepper, and seasoning, or by shaking thoroughly in a screw-topped jar.

Pour 2 tablespoons of the dressing over the salad and toss well. Turn into a serving dish and sprinkle the toasted sesame seeds and chopped parsley on top. Serve the remaining dressing separately.

Try this: FOR AN ALTERNATIVE: 306 FOR KIDS: 20

Panzanella

SERVES 4

1 tbsp red wine vinegar
12 slices day-old,
   Italian-style bread
4 tbsp olive oil
1 tsp lemon juice
1 small garlic clove, peeled
   and finely chopped

1 red onion, peeled and
   finely sliced
1 cucumber, peeled
   if preferred
2 medium ripe tomatoes,
   deseeded
32–36 pitted black olives

about 20 basil leaves,
   coarsely torn or left
   whole if small
sea salt and freshly ground
   black pepper

Add 1 teaspoon of red wine vinegar to a jug of iced water, put the slices of bread in a bowl, and pour the water over them. Make sure the bread is covered completely. Let soak for 3–4 minutes until just soft.

Remove the soaked bread from the water and squeeze it gently, first with your hands and then in a clean kitchen towel to remove any excess water. Put the bread on a plate, cover with plastic wrap, and chill in the refrigerator for about 1 hour.

Meanwhile, whisk together the olive oil, the remaining red wine vinegar, and lemon juice in a large serving bowl. Add the garlic and onion and stir to coat well.

Halve the cucumber and remove the seeds. Chop both the cucumber and tomatoes into ½-inch cubes. Add to the garlic and onions with the olives. Tear the bread into bite-sized chunks and add to the bowl with the fresh basil leaves. Toss together to mix and serve immediately, with a grinding of sea salt and black pepper.

Try this: FOR AN ALTERNATIVE: 330 FOR KIDS: 334

Oriental Noodle & Peanut Salad with Cilantro

SERVES 4

12 oz rice vermicelli (noodles)
4¼ cups light chicken stock
2 tsp sesame oil
2 tbsp light soy sauce
8 green onions
3 tbsp peanut oil

2 hot green chile peppers,
    deseeded and thinly
    sliced
4 tbsp roughly chopped
    cilantro
2 tbsp freshly chopped mint

½ medium cucumber,
    finely chopped
⅓ cup bean sprouts
4½ tbsp roasted peanuts,
    roughly chopped

Put the noodles into a large bowl. Bring the stock to a boil and immediately pour over the noodles. Let soak for 4 minutes, or according to the package directions. Drain well, discarding the stock or saving it for another use. Mix together the sesame oil and soy sauce and pour over the hot noodles. Toss well to coat and let stand until cold.

Trim and thinly slice four of the green onions. Heat the oil in a wok over a low heat. Add the green onions and, as soon as they sizzle, remove from the heat and let cool. When cold, toss with the noodles.

On a cutting board, cut the remaining green onions lengthways four to six times, and let stand in a bowl of cold water until tassels form. Serve the noodles in individual bowls, each dressed with a little chile pepper, cilantro, mint, cucumber, bean sprouts, and peanuts. Garnish with the green onion tassels and serve.

Try this: FOR AN ALTERNATIVE: 338   FOR KIDS: 52

Vegetable Thai Egg Rolls

SERVES 4

2 oz cellophane vermicelli
4 dried shiitake mushrooms
1 tbsp peanut oil
2 medium carrots, peeled
    and cut into fine
    matchsticks
1½ cups snow peas, cut
    lengthways into fine strips
3 green onions, trimmed

and chopped
4-oz can bamboo shoots, cut
    into fine matchsticks
½-inch piece fresh ginger,
    peeled and grated
1 tbsp light soy sauce
1 medium egg, separated
salt and freshly ground
    black pepper

20 egg roll wrappers, each
    about 5-inch square
vegetable oil for deep-frying
green onion tassels,
    to garnish

Place the vermicelli in a bowl and pour over enough boiling water to cover. Let soak for 5 minutes, or until softened, then drain. Cut into 3-inch lengths. Soak the shiitake mushrooms in almost boiling water for 15 minutes, drain, discard the stalks, and slice thinly. Heat a wok or large skillet and add the peanut oil; when hot, add the carrots and stir-fry for 1 minute. Add the snow peas and green onions and stir-fry for 2–3 minutes, or until tender. Tip the vegetables into a bowl and let cool. Stir the vermicelli and shiitake mushrooms into the cooled vegetables with the bamboo shoots, ginger, soy sauce, and egg yolk. Season to taste with salt and pepper and mix thoroughly.

Brush the edges of an egg roll wrapper with a little beaten egg white. Spoon 2 teaspoons of the vegetable filling onto the wrapper, in a 3-inch log shape, 1 inch from one edge. Fold the wrapper edge over the filling, then fold in the right and left sides. Brush the folded edges with more egg white and roll up neatly. Place on an oiled baking sheet, seam-side down, and make the rest of the egg rolls. Heat the oil in a heavy-based saucepan or deep-fat fryer to 350°F. Deep-fry the egg rolls, six at a time for 2–3 minutes, or until golden brown and crisp. Drain on a paper towel and arrange on a warmed platter. Garnish with green onion tassels (see page 306) and serve immediately.

Try this: FOR AN ALTERNATIVE: 194 FOR KIDS: 164

Pumpkin Pâté

SERVES 8-10

1 lb fresh pumpkin flesh,
  peeled, or 15–oz can
  pumpkin puree
1 tsp sunflower oil
1 small onion, peeled
  and finely chopped
½ orange bell pepper,
  deseeded and

finely chopped
2 medium eggs, beaten
3 tbsp plain yogurt
1 cup hard cheese, such
  as Edam, Cheddar, or
  Gouda, grated
½ cup wheat germ
1 tbsp freshly

chopped oregano
salt and freshly ground
  black pepper
fresh lettuce leaves and
  crusty bread, to serve

Preheat the oven to 350˚F. Oil and line a loaf pan. Cut the pumpkin flesh into cubes and place in a pan of boiling water. Simmer for 20 minutes or until the pumpkin is tender. Drain and let cool, then mash well to form a puree.

Heat the oil in a nonstick skillet and cook the chopped onion and pepper for about 4 minutes, until softened. Mix together the pureed pumpkin, softened vegetables, eggs, and yogurt. Add the cheese, wheat germ, and chopped oregano. Season well with salt and pepper.

When the pumpkin mixture is well blended, spoon it into the prepared pan and stand in a baking dish. Fill the baking dish with hot water to come halfway up the sides of the dish and carefully place in the preheated oven.

Bake for about 1 hour or until firm, then let cool. Chill for 30 minutes before turning out onto a serving plate. Serve with crusty bread and a fresh salad.

Try this: FOR AN ALTERNATIVE: 314   FOR KIDS: 294

Hot Herb Mushrooms

SERVES 4

4 thin slices of white bread,
   crusts removed
1½ cups mushrooms,
   cleaned and sliced
1½ cups oyster mushrooms,
   cleaned
1 garlic clove, peeled

and crushed
1 tsp Dijon mustard
1¼ cups chicken stock
salt and freshly ground
   black pepper
1 tbsp freshly
   chopped parsley

1 tbsp freshly snipped
   chives, plus extra
   to garnish
mixed lettuce leaves,
   to serve

Preheat the oven to 350°F. With a rolling pin, roll each piece of bread out as thinly as possible. Press each piece of bread into a 4-inch tartlet pan. Push each piece firmly down, then bake in the preheated oven for 20 minutes.

Place the mushrooms in a skillet with the garlic, mustard, and chicken stock, and stir-fry over a moderate heat until the mushrooms are tender and the liquid is reduced by half.

Carefully remove the mushrooms from the skillet with a slatted spoon and transfer to a heat-resistant dish. Cover with foil and place in the bottom of the oven to keep the mushrooms warm.

Boil the remaining pan juices until reduced to a thick sauce. Season with salt and pepper. Stir the parsley and the chives into the mushroom mixture.

Place one bread tartlet shell on each plate and divide the mushroom mixture between them. Spoon over the pan juices, garnish with the chives, and serve immediately with mixed lettuce leaves.

Mushroom & Red Wine Pâté

SERVES 4

3 large slices of white bread,
   crusts removed
2 tsp oil
1 small onion, peeled and
   finely chopped
1 garlic clove, peeled
   and crushed

5 cups mushrooms, cleaned
   and finely chopped
⅔ cup red wine
½ tsp dried mixed herbs
1 tbsp freshly
   chopped parsley
salt and freshly ground

black pepper
2 tbsp cream cheese

To serve:
finely chopped cucumber
finely chopped tomato

Preheat the oven to 350°F. Cut the bread in half diagonally. Place the bread triangles on a baking sheet and cook for 10 minutes. Remove from the oven and split each bread triangle in half to make 12 triangles, then return to the oven until golden and crisp. Let cool on a wire rack.

Heat the oil in a saucepan and gently cook the onion and garlic until transparent. Add the mushrooms and cook, stirring for 3–4 minutes, or until the mushroom juices start to run.

Stir the wine and herbs into the mushroom mixture and bring to a boil. Reduce the heat and simmer, uncovered, until all the liquid is absorbed. Remove from the heat and season to taste with salt and pepper. Let cool.

When cold, beat in the cream cheese and adjust the seasoning. Place in a small, clean bowl and chill until required. Serve with the toast triangles and the cucumber and tomato.

Try this: FOR AN ALTERNATIVE: 38   FOR KIDS: 310

Roasted Eggplant Dip
with Pita Strips

SERVES 4

4 pita breads
2 large eggplants
1 garlic clove, peeled
¼ tsp sesame oil

1 tbsp lemon juice
½ tsp ground cumin
salt and freshly ground
    black pepper

2 tbsp freshly
    chopped parsley
fresh lettuce leaves,
    to serve

Preheat the oven to 350°F. On a cutting board cut the pita breads into strips. Spread the bread in a single layer onto a large baking sheet. Cook in the preheated oven for 15 minutes, until golden and crisp. Let cool on a wire cooling rack.

Trim the eggplants, rinse lightly, and reserve. Heat a griddle pan until almost smoking. Cook the eggplants and garlic for about 15 minutes. Turn the eggplants frequently, until tender with wrinkled and charred skins. Remove from the heat and let cool.

When the eggplants are cool enough to handle, cut in half and scoop out the cooked flesh and place in a food processor. Squeeze the softened garlic flesh from the papery skin and add to the eggplant.

Blend the eggplant and garlic until smooth, then add the sesame oil, lemon juice, and cumin and blend again to mix. Season to taste with salt and pepper, stir in the parsley, and serve with the pita strips and mixed lettuce leaves.

Wild Rice Dolmades

SERVES 4-6

6 tbsp olive oil
3 tbsp pine nuts
2½ cups mushrooms,
    cleaned and finely
    chopped
4 green onions, trimmed
    and finely chopped

1 garlic clove, peeled
    and crushed
1¼ cups cooked wild rice
2 tsp freshly chopped dill
2 tsp freshly chopped mint
salt and freshly ground
    black pepper

16–24 prepared medium
    vine leaves
1¼ cups vegetable stock

To garnish:
lemon wedges
sprigs of fresh dill

Heat 1 tbsp of the oil in a skillet and gently cook the pine nuts for 2–3 minutes, stirring frequently, until golden. Remove from the skillet and reserve.

Add 1½ tablespoons of oil to the skillet and gently cook the mushrooms, green onions, and garlic for 7–8 minutes, until soft. Stir in the rice, herbs, salt, and pepper.

Put a heaped teaspoon of stuffing in the center of each vine leaf – if the leaves are small put two together, overlapping slightly. Fold over the stalk end, then the sides, and roll up to make a neat parcel. Continue until all the stuffing is used.

Arrange the stuffed vine leaves close together, seam-side down, in a large saucepan, drizzling each with a little of the remaining oil – there will be several layers. Pour over just enough stock to cover. Put an inverted plate over the dolmades to stop them unrolling during cooking. Bring to a boil, then simmer gently for 3 minutes. Cool in the saucepan.

Transfer the dolmades to a serving dish. Cover and chill in the refrigerator before serving. Sprinkle with the pine nuts and garnish with lemon and dill. Serve.

Try this: FOR AN ALTERNATIVE: 286 FOR KIDS: 138

Roasted Mixed Vegetables with Garlic & Herb Sauce

SERVES 4

1 large garlic bulb
1 large onion, peeled
   and cut into wedges
4 small carrots, peeled
   and quartered
4 small parsnips, peeled
6 small potatoes, scrubbed
   and halved
1 fennel bulb, sliced thickly
4 sprigs of fresh rosemary
4 sprigs of fresh thyme
2 tbsp olive oil
salt and freshly ground
   black pepper
1 cup soft cheese with herbs
   and garlic
4 tbsp milk
zest of ½ lemon
sprigs of thyme, to garnish

Preheat the oven to 425˚F. Cut the garlic in half horizontally. Put into a large roasting pan with all the vegetables and herbs. Add the oil, season well with salt and pepper, and toss together to coat lightly in the oil.

Cover with foil and roast in the preheated oven for 50 minutes. Remove the foil and cook for a further 30 minutes, until all the vegetables are tender and slightly charred. Remove the pan from the oven and let cool.

In a small saucepan, melt the soft cheese together with the milk and lemon zest.

Remove the garlic from the roasting pan and squeeze the flesh into a bowl. Mash thoroughly, then add to the sauce. Heat through gently.

Season the vegetables to taste. Pour some sauce into small ramekins and garnish with four sprigs of thyme. Serve immediately with the roasted vegetables and the sauce to dip.

Try this: FOR AN ALTERNATIVE: 338   FOR KIDS: 182

Spanish Baked Tomatoes

SERVES 4

1 cup brown rice
600 ml/1 pint
    vegetable stock
2 tsp sunflower oil
2 shallots, peeled and
    finely chopped
1 garlic clove, peeled
    and crushed

1 green bell pepper,
    deseeded and diced
1 red chile pepper, deseeded
    and finely chopped
¾ cup mushrooms, finely
    chopped
1 tbsp freshly
    chopped oregano

salt and freshly ground
    black pepper
4 large ripe beef tomatoes
1 large egg, beaten
1 tsp superfine sugar
basil leaves, to garnish
crusty bread, to serve

Preheat the oven to 350°F. Place the rice in a saucepan, add the vegetable stock, and bring to a boil. Simmer for 30 minutes, or until the rice is tender. Drain and turn into a mixing bowl.

Add 1 teaspoon of sunflower oil to a small, nonstick pan and gently fry the shallots, garlic, pepper, chile pepper, and mushrooms for 2 minutes. Add to the rice with the chopped oregano. Season with plenty of salt and pepper.

Slice the top off each tomato. Cut and scoop out the flesh, removing the hard core. Pass the tomato flesh through a sieve. Add 1 tablespoon of the juice to the rice mixture. Stir in the beaten egg and mix. Sprinkle a little sugar in the base of each tomato. Pile the rice mixture into the shells.

Place the tomatoes in a baking dish and pour a little cold water around them. Replace their lids and drizzle a few drops of sunflower oil over the tops. Bake in the preheated oven for about 25 minutes. Garnish with the basil leaves, season with black pepper, and serve immediately with crusty bread.

   Try this: FOR AN ALTERNATIVE: 278   FOR KIDS: 346

Sweet Corn Fritters

SERVES 4

4 tbsp peanut oil
1 small onion, peeled and
    finely chopped
1 red chile pepper, deseeded
    and finely chopped
1 garlic clove, peeled
    and crushed

1 tsp ground coriander
11½-oz can corn kernels
6 green onions, trimmed
    and finely sliced
1 medium egg,
    lightly beaten
salt and freshly ground

black pepper
3 tbsp all-purpose flour
1 tsp baking powder
green onion curls,
    to garnish
Thai-style chutney,
    to serve

Heat 1 tablespoon of the peanut oil in a skillet, add the onion, and cook gently for 7–8 minutes, or until beginning to soften. Add the chile pepper, garlic, and ground coriander and cook for 1 minute, stirring continuously. Remove from the heat.

Drain the corn kernels and tip into a mixing bowl. Lightly mash with a potato masher to break down the kernels a little. Add the cooked onion mixture to the bowl with the green onions and beaten egg. Season to taste with salt and pepper, then stir to mix together. Sift the flour and baking powder over the mixture and stir in.

Heat 2 tablespoons of the peanut oil in a large skillet. Drop four or five heaped teaspoonfuls of the corn mixture into the pan, and, using a spatula, flatten each to make a ½-inch thick fritter.

Fry the fritters for 3 minutes, or until golden brown on the underside, turn over, and fry for a further 3 minutes, or until cooked through and crisp.

Remove the fritters from the skillet and drain on a paper towel. Keep warm while cooking the remaining fritters, adding a little more oil if needed. Garnish with green onion curls (see page 306) and serve immediately with a Thai-style chutney.

Try this: FOR AN ALTERNATIVE: 118   FOR KIDS: 62

Spinach & Mushroom Wontons

MAKES 15

4 oz phyllo dough or
    wonton skins
15 whole chive leaves
8 cups spinach
2 tbsp butter
½ tsp salt
3¼ cups mushrooms,
    cleaned and chopped

1 garlic clove, peeled and
    crushed
1–2 tbsp dark soy sauce
1-inch piece fresh ginger,
    peeled and grated
salt and freshly ground
    black pepper
1 small egg, beaten

1¼ cups peanut oil for deep-
    frying

To garnish:
green onion curls
radish roses

Cut the phyllo dough or wonton skins into 5-inch squares, stack, and cover with plastic wrap. Chill in the refrigerator while preparing the filling. Blanch the chive leaves in boiling water for 1 minute, drain, and reserve.

Melt the butter in a saucepan, add the spinach and salt, and cook for 2–3 minutes, or until wilted. Add the mushrooms and garlic and cook for 2–3 minutes, or until tender. Transfer the spinach and mushroom mixture to a bowl. Stir in the soy sauce and ginger. Season to taste with salt and pepper.

Place a small spoonful of the spinach and mushroom mixture onto a pastry or wonton square and brush the edges with beaten egg. Gather up the four corners to make a little bag and tie with a chive leaf. Make up the remainder of the wontons.

Heat a wok, add the oil, and heat to 350°F. Deep-fry the wontons in batches for 2–3 minutes, or until golden and crisp. Drain on a paper towel and serve immediately, garnished with green onion curls (see page 306) and radish roses.

Try this: FOR AN ALTERNATIVE: 60   FOR KIDS: 298

Baby Roast Potato Salad

SERVES 4

30 small shallots
(about 12 oz)
sea salt and freshly ground
black pepper
18–24 small new potatoes

(about 2 lb)
2 tbsp olive oil
2 medium zucchini
2 sprigs of fresh rosemary
10 cherry tomatoes

⅔ cup sour cream
2 tbsp freshly
snipped chives
¼ tsp paprika

Preheat the oven to 400°F. Trim the shallots, but leave the skins on. Put in a saucepan of lightly salted boiling water with the potatoes and cook for 5 minutes, then drain. Separate the shallots and plunge them into cold water for 1 minute.

Put the oil on a baking sheet or roasting pan lined with foil and heat for a few minutes. Peel the skins off the shallots – they should now come away easily. Add to the baking sheet or roasting pan with the potatoes and toss in the oil to coat. Sprinkle with a little sea salt. Roast the potatoes and shallots in the preheated oven for 10 minutes.

Meanwhile, trim the zucchini, halve lengthways, and cut into 2-inch chunks. Add to the baking sheet or roasting pan, toss to mix, and cook for 5 minutes.

Pierce the tomato skins with a sharp knife. Add to the baking sheet or roasting pan with the rosemary and cook for a further 5 minutes, or until all the vegetables are tender. Remove the rosemary and discard. Grind a little black pepper over the vegetables.

Spoon into a wide serving bowl. Mix together the sour cream, chives, and paprika and drizzle over the vegetables just before serving.

Try this: FOR AN ALTERNATIVE: 280 FOR KIDS: 266

Sicilian Baked Eggplant

SERVES 4

1 large eggplant, trimmed
2 celery stalks, trimmed
4 large ripe tomatoes
1 tsp sunflower oil
2 shallots, peeled and
    finely chopped

1½ tsp tomato paste
5 large, pitted green olives
5 large, pitted black olives
salt and freshly ground
    black pepper
1 tbsp white wine vinegar

2 tsp superfine sugar
1 tbsp freshly chopped basil,
    to garnish
mixed lettuce leaves,
    to serve

Preheat the oven to 400°F. Cut the eggplant into small cubes and place on an oiled baking sheet. Cover the sheet with foil and bake in the preheated oven for 15–20 minutes, until soft. Reserve, letting the eggplant cool.

Place the celery and tomatoes in a large bowl and cover with boiling water. Remove the tomatoes from the bowl when their skins begin to peel away. Remove the skins, then deseed and chop the flesh into small pieces. Remove the celery from the bowl of water, finely chop, and reserve.

Pour the vegetable oil into a nonstick saucepan, add the chopped shallots, and fry gently for 2–3 minutes, until soft. Add the celery, tomatoes, tomato paste, and olives. Season to taste with salt and pepper.

Simmer gently for 3–4 minutes. Add the vinegar, sugar, and cooled eggplant to the pan and heat gently for 2–3 minutes, until all the ingredients are well blended. Reserve to let the eggplant mixture cool. When cool, garnish with the chopped basil and serve cold with lettuce leaves.

Try this: FOR AN ALTERNATIVE: 350 FOR KIDS: 294

Pasta with Zucchini, Rosemary, & Lemon

SERVES 4

12 oz dried pasta shapes,
  such as rigatoni
1½ tbsp good quality
  extra virgin olive oil
2 garlic cloves, peeled
  and finely chopped
4 medium zucchini,
  thinly sliced

1 tbsp freshly
  chopped rosemary
1 tbsp freshly
  chopped parsley
zest and juice of 2 lemons
5 large, pitted black olives,
  roughly chopped
5 large, pitted green olives,

roughly chopped
salt and freshly ground
  black pepper

To garnish:
lemon slices
sprigs of fresh rosemary

Bring a large saucepan of salted water to a boil and add the pasta. Return to a boil and cook until firm but cooked, or according to the package instructions.

When the pasta is almost cooked, heat the oil in a large skillet and add the garlic. Cook over a medium heat until the garlic just begins to brown. Be careful not to overcook the garlic or it will become bitter.

Add the zucchini, rosemary, parsley, and lemon zest and juice. Cook for 3–4 minutes, until the zucchini is just tender.

Add the olives to the skillet and stir well. Season to taste with salt and pepper and remove from the heat.

Drain the pasta well and add to the skillet. Stir until thoroughly combined. Garnish with lemon and sprigs of fresh rosemary and serve immediately.

Try this: FOR AN ALTERNATIVE: 96 FOR KIDS: 290

Rice Nuggets in Herb Tomato Sauce

SERVES 4

2½ cups vegetable stock
1 bay leaf
1 cup arborio or risotto rice
½ cup Cheddar
   cheese, grated
1 medium egg yolk
1 tbsp all-purpose flour
2 tbsp freshly

chopped parsley
salt and freshly ground
   black pepper
grated Parmesan cheese,
   to serve

For the herb tomato sauce:
1 tbsp olive oil

1 onion, peeled and
   thinly sliced
1 garlic clove, peeled
   and crushed
1 small yellow bell pepper,
   deseeded and diced
14-oz can chopped tomatoes
1 tbsp freshly chopped basil

Pour the stock into a large saucepan. Add the bay leaf. Bring to a boil, add the rice, stir, then cover and simmer for 15 minutes. Uncover, reduce the heat to low, and cook for a further 5 minutes, until the rice is tender and all the stock is absorbed, stirring frequently toward the end of the cooking time. Let cool.

Stir the cheese, egg yolk, flour, and parsley into the rice. Season to taste, then shape into 20 walnut-sized balls. Cover and refrigerate.

To make the sauce, heat the oil in a large skillet and cook the onion for 5 minutes. Add the garlic and yellow bell pepper, and cook for a further 5 minutes, until soft. Stir in the chopped tomatoes and simmer gently for 3 minutes. Stir in the chopped basil and season to taste.

Add the rice nuggets to the sauce and simmer for a further 10 minutes, or until the rice nuggets are cooked through and the sauce has reduced a little. Spoon onto serving plates and serve hot, sprinkled with grated Parmesan cheese.

Stuffed Onions with Pine Nuts

SERVES 4

4 medium onions, peeled
2 garlic cloves, peeled
   and crushed
2 tbsp fresh
   brown bread crumbs
2 tbsp white bread crumbs

3 tbsp golden raisins
3 tbsp pine nuts
½ cup hard cheese,
   such as Edam or
   Cheddar, grated
2 tbsp freshly

chopped parsley
1 medium egg, beaten
salt and freshly ground
   black pepper
salad leaves, to serve

Preheat the oven to 400°F. Bring a saucepan of water to a boil, add the onions, and cook gently for about 15 minutes.

Drain well. Let the onions cool, then slice each one in half horizontally. Scoop out most of the onion flesh but leave a reasonably firm shell.

Chop up 4 tablespoons of the onion flesh and place in a bowl with the crushed garlic, bread crumbs, golden raisins, pine nuts, parsley and most of the grated cheese.

Mix the bread crumb mixture together thoroughly. Bind together with as much of the beaten egg as necessary to make a firm filling. Season to taste with salt and pepper.

Pile the mixture back into the onion shells and top with the rest of the grated cheese. Place on a oiled baking sheet and cook in the preheated oven for 20–30 minutes, or until golden brown. Serve immediately with the lettuce leaves.

 Try this: FOR AN ALTERNATIVE: 152 FOR KIDS: 318

Cooked Vegetable Salad with Satay Sauce

SERVES 4

½ cup peanut oil
1½ cups unsalted peanuts
1 onion, peeled and
  finely chopped
1 garlic clove, peeled
  and crushed
½ tsp chile powder
1 tsp ground coriander
½ tsp ground cumin
½ tsp sugar

1 tbsp dark soy sauce
2 tbsp fresh lemon juice
2 tbsp light olive oil
salt and freshly ground
  black pepper
1 cup green beans, trimmed
  and halved
1 large carrot
½ cup cauliflower florets
½ cup broccoli florets

⅔ cup Chinese cabbage or
  pak choi, trimmed and
  shredded
¾ cup bean sprouts
1 tbsp sesame oil

To garnish:
sprigs of fresh watercress
cucumber, cut into slivers

Heat a wok and add the oil; when hot, add the peanuts and stir-fry for 3–4 minutes. Drain on a paper towel and let cool. Blend in a food processor to a fine powder.

Place the onion and garlic, with the spices, sugar, soy sauce, lemon juice, and olive oil in a food processor. Season to taste with salt and pepper, then process into a paste. Transfer to a wok and stir-fry for 3–4 minutes.

Stir 2½ cups of hot water into the paste and bring to a boil. Add the ground peanuts and simmer gently for 5–6 minutes, or until the mixture thickens. Reserve the satay sauce.

Cook the vegetables in batches in lightly salted boiling water. Cook the green beans, carrots, cauliflower, and broccoli for 3–4 minutes, and the Chinese cabbage or pak choi and bean sprouts for 2 minutes. Drain each batch, drizzle over the sesame oil, and arrange on a large, warmed serving dish. Garnish with watercress sprigs and cucumber. Serve with the satay sauce.

Bulgur Wheat Salad with Minty Lemon Dressing

SERVES 4

⅔ cup bulgur wheat
4-inch piece cucumber
2 shallots, peeled
24 baby sweet corn
3 firm, ripe tomatoes

For the dressing:
grated rind of 1 lemon
3 tbsp lemon juice
3 tbsp freshly chopped mint
2 tbsp freshly
    chopped parsley

1–2 tsp clear honey
2 tbsp sunflower oil
salt and freshly ground
    black pepper

Place the bulgur wheat in a saucepan and cover with boiling water. Simmer for about 10 minutes, then drain thoroughly and turn into a serving bowl.

Cut the cucumber into small cubes, chop the shallots finely, and reserve. Steam the sweet corn over a pan of boiling water for 10 minutes, or until tender. Drain and slice in to thick chunks.

Cut a cross on the top of each tomato and place in boiling water until their skins start to peel away. Remove the skins and the seeds and cut the tomatoes into small cubes.

Make the dressing by briskly whisking all the ingredients in a small bowl until mixed well. When the bulgur wheat has cooled, add all the prepared vegetables and stir in the dressing. Season to taste with salt and pepper and serve.

Try this: FOR AN ALTERNATIVE: 272 FOR KIDS: 254

Red Lentil Kedgeree
with Avocado & Tomatoes

SERVES 4

¾ cup basmati rice
¾ cup red lentils
1 tbsp butter
1 tbsp sunflower oil
1 medium onion, peeled
   and chopped
1 tsp ground cumin
4 cardamom pods, bruised

1 bay leaf
2 cups vegetable stock
1 ripe avocado, peeled,
   stoned, and diced
1 tbsp lemon juice
4 plum tomatoes,
   peeled and diced
2 tbsp freshly

chopped cilantro
salt and freshly ground
   black pepper
lemon or lime slices,
   to garnish

Put the rice and lentils in a sieve and rinse under cold running water. Tip into a bowl, then pour over enough cold water to cover and let soak for 10 minutes.

Heat the butter and oil in a saucepan. Add the sliced onion and cook gently, stirring occasionally, for 10 minutes, until softened. Stir in the cumin, cardamom pods, and bay leaf and cook for a further minute, stirring all the time.

Drain the rice and lentils, rinse again, and add to the onions in the saucepan. Stir in the vegetable stock and bring to a boil. Reduce the heat, cover the saucepan, and simmer for 14–15 minutes, or until the rice and lentils are tender.

Place the diced avocado in a bowl and toss with the lemon juice. Stir in the tomatoes and chopped cilantro. Season to taste with salt and pepper.

Fluff up the rice with a fork, spoon into a warmed serving dish, and spoon the avocado mixture on top. Garnish with lemon or lime slices and serve.

Try this: FOR AN ALTERNATIVE: 378   FOR KIDS: 36

Cheese–crusted Potato Scones

MAKES 6

1¾ cups all-purpose flour
¼ cup whole-grain flour
½ tsp salt
1½ tsp baking powder
2 tbsp butter, cubed
5 tbsp milk

1 cup cold mashed potato
freshly ground black pepper

To finish:
2 tbsp milk
6 tbsp mature Cheddar

cheese, finely grated
paprika, to dust
sprig of basil, to garnish

Preheat the oven to 425°F 15 minutes before baking. Sift the flours, salt, and baking powder into a large bowl. Rub in the butter until the mixture resembles fine bread crumbs.

Stir 4 tablespoons of the milk into the mashed potato and season with black pepper. Add the dry ingredients to the potato mixture, mixing together with a fork and adding the remaining 1 tablespoon of milk if needed.

Knead the dough on a lightly floured surface for a few seconds until smooth. Roll out to a 6-inch round and transfer to an oiled baking sheet.

Mark the scone round into six wedges, cutting about halfway through with a small sharp knife. Brush with milk, then sprinkle with the cheese and a faint dusting of paprika.

Bake on the middle shelf of the preheated oven for 15 minutes, or until well risen and golden brown. Transfer to a wire rack and let cool for 5 minutes before breaking into wedges.

Serve warm or let cool completely. Once cool, store the scones in an airtight container. Garnish with a sprig of basil and serve split and buttered.

Try this: FOR AN ALTERNATIVE: 348   FOR KIDS: 284

Spinach Dumplings with Rich Tomato Sauce

SERVES 4

For the sauce:
2 tbsp olive oil
1 onion, peeled
   and chopped
1 garlic clove, peeled
   and crushed
1 red chile pepper, deseeded
   and chopped
⅔ cup dry white wine
14–oz can chopped

tomatoes
pared strip of lemon rind

For the dumplings:
1 lb fresh spinach
3 tbsp ricotta cheese
½ cup fresh white bread
   crumbs
¼ cup Parmesan
   cheese, grated

1 medium egg yolk
¼ tsp freshly
   grated nutmeg
salt and freshly ground
   black pepper
5 tbsp all-purpose flour
2 tbsp olive oil, for frying
fresh basil leaves, to garnish
freshly cooked tagliatelle,
   to serve

To make the tomato sauce, heat the olive oil in a large saucepan and fry the onion gently for 5 minutes. Add the garlic and chile pepper and cook for a further 5 minutes, until softened. Stir in the wine, chopped tomatoes, and lemon rind. Bring to a boil, cover, and simmer for 20 minutes, then uncover and simmer for 15 minutes, or until the sauce has thickened. Remove the lemon rind and season to taste with salt and pepper.

To make the spinach dumplings, wash the spinach thoroughly and remove any tough stalks. Cover and cook in a large saucepan over a low heat with the water just clinging to the leaves. Drain, then squeeze out all the excess water. Finely chop and put in a large bowl.

Add the ricotta, bread crumbs, Parmesan cheese, and egg yolk to the spinach. Season with nutmeg and salt and pepper. Mix together and shape into 20 walnut-sized balls.

Toss the spinach balls in the flour. Heat the olive oil in a large, nonstick skillet and fry the balls gently for 5–6 minutes, carefully turning occasionally. Garnish with fresh basil leaves and serve immediately with the tomato sauce and tagliatelle.

Try this: FOR AN ALTERNATIVE: 184   FOR KIDS: 334

Rosemary & Olive Focaccia

MAKES 2 LOAVES

6 cups all-purpose flour
pinch of salt
pinch of caster sugar
1 tbsp dried yeast
2 tsp freshly
   chopped rosemary

2 cups warm water
3 tbsp olive oil
15 large, pitted black olives,
   roughly chopped
sprigs of rosemary,
   to garnish

To finish:
3 tbsp olive oil
coarse sea salt
freshly ground black pepper

Preheat the oven to 400°F 15 minutes before baking. Sift the flour, salt, and sugar into a large bowl. Stir in the yeast and rosemary. Make a well in the center. Pour in the warm water and the oil and mix to a soft dough. Turn out on to a lightly floured surface and knead for about 10 minutes, until smooth and elastic.

Pat the olives dry on a paper towel, then gently knead into the dough. Put in an oiled bowl, cover with plastic wrap, and let rise in a warm place for 1½ hours, or until it has doubled in size. Turn out the dough and knead again for a minute or two. Divide in half and roll out each piece to a 10-inch circle.

Transfer to oiled baking sheets, cover with oiled plastic wrap, and let rise for 30 minutes. Using your fingertips, make deep dimples all over the dough. Drizzle with the oil and sprinkle with sea salt.

Bake in the preheated oven for 20–25 minutes, or until risen and golden. Cool on a wire rack and garnish with sprigs of rosemary. Grind over a little black pepper before serving.

Try this: FOR AN ALTERNATIVE: 344 FOR KIDS: 164

Warm Leek & Tomato Salad

SERVES 4

1 bunch baby leeks
(about 1 lb)
2 medium firm, ripe
tomatoes
2 shallots, peeled and cut
into thin wedges

For the honey and
lime dressing:
2 tbsp clear honey
grated rind of 1 lime
4 tbsp lime juice
1 tbsp light olive oil

1 tsp Dijon mustard
salt and freshly ground
black pepper
freshly chopped tarragon
and freshly chopped basil,
to garnish

Trim the leeks so that they are all the same length. Place in a steamer over a pan of boiling water and steam for 8 minutes, or until just tender. Drain the leeks thoroughly and arrange in a shallow serving dish.

Make a cross in the top of the tomatoes, place in a bowl, and cover them with boiling water until their skins start to peel away. Remove from the bowl and carefully remove the skins.

Cut the tomatoes into four and remove the seeds, then chop into small cubes. Spoon over the top of the leeks, together with the shallots.

In a small bowl, make the dressing by whisking the honey, lime rind, lime juice, olive oil, mustard, and salt and pepper. Pour 3 tablespoons of the dressing over the leeks and tomatoes and garnish with the tarragon and basil. Serve while the leeks are still warm, with the remaining dressing served separately.

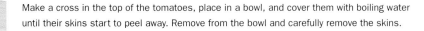

Try this: FOR AN ALTERNATIVE: 136   FOR KIDS: 328

Chinese Salad with Soy & Ginger Dressing

SERVES 4

1 head of Chinese cabbage
7-oz can water
    chestnuts, drained
6 green onions, trimmed
4 firm, ripe cherry tomatoes
1½ cups snow peas
¾ cup bean sprouts

2 tbsp freshly
    chopped cilantro

For the soy and ginger
    dressing:
2 tbsp sunflower oil
4 tbsp light soy sauce

1-inch piece fresh ginger,
    peeled and finely grated
zest and juice of 1 lemon
salt and black pepper
crusty white bread, to serve

Rinse and finely shred the Chinese cabbage and place in a serving dish. Slice the water chestnuts into small slivers and cut the green onions diagonally into 1-inch lengths, then split lengthwise into thin strips.

Cut the tomatoes in half, then slice each half into three wedges and reserve. Simmer the snow peas in boiling water for 2 minutes until they begin to soften; drain, and cut in half diagonally.

Arrange the water chestnuts, green onions, snow peas, tomatoes, and bean sprouts on top of the shredded Chinese cabbage. Garnish with the freshly chopped cilantro.

Make the dressing by whisking all the ingredients together in a small bowl until mixed thoroughly. Serve with the bread and the salad.

Try this: FOR AN ALTERNATIVE: 306   FOR KIDS: 194

Marinated Vegetable Kebabs

SERVES 4

2 small zucchini, cut into
⅜-inch pieces
½ green bell pepper,
deseeded and cut into
1-inch pieces
½ red bell pepper,
deseeded and cut into
1-inch pieces
½ yellow bell pepper,
deseeded and cut into
1-inch pieces

8 baby onions, peeled
8 mushrooms
8 cherry tomatoes
freshly chopped parsley,
to garnish
freshly cooked couscous,
to serve

For the marinade:
1 tbsp light olive oil
4 tbsp dry sherry
2 tbsp light soy sauce
1 red chile pepper, deseeded
and finely chopped
2 garlic cloves, peeled
and crushed
1-inch piece fresh ginger,
peeled and finely grated

Place the zucchini, peppers, and baby onions in a pan of just boiled water. Bring back to a boil and simmer for about 30 seconds. Drain and rinse the cooked vegetables in cold water and dry on a paper towel.

Thread the cooked vegetables and the mushrooms and tomatoes alternately onto skewers and place in a large shallow dish.

Make the marinade by whisking all the ingredients together until thoroughly blended. Pour the marinade evenly over the kebabs, then chill in the refrigerator for at least 1 hour. Spoon the marinade over the kebabs occasionally during this time.

Place the kebabs in a hot griddle pan or on a hot barbecue and cook gently for 10–12 minutes. Turn the kebabs frequently and brush with the marinade when needed. When the vegetables are tender, sprinkle over the chopped parsley and serve immediately with couscous.

Try this: FOR AN ALTERNATIVE: 296   FOR KIDS: 142

Caramelized Fennel & Shallot Tartlets

SERVES 6

For the cheese pastry:
1½ cups all-purpose flour
6 tbsp slightly
    salted butter
½ cup Gruyère
    cheese, grated
1 small egg yolk

For the filling:
2 tbsp olive oil
8–12 medium shallots (about
    8 oz), peeled and halved
1 fennel bulb, trimmed
    and sliced
1 tsp brown sugar
1 medium egg

⅔ cup heavy cream
salt and freshly ground
    black pepper
¼ cup Gruyère cheese,
    grated
½ tsp ground cinnamon
mixed lettuce leaves,
    to serve

Preheat the oven to 400°F. Sift the flour into a bowl, then rub in the butter using your fingertips. Stir in the cheese, then add the egg yolk with about 2 tablespoons of cold water. Mix to a firm dough, then knead lightly. Wrap in plastic wrap and chill in the refrigerator for 30 minutes.

Roll out the pastry on a lightly floured surface and use to line six 4-inch individual flan pans or muffin pans that are about ¾ inch deep. Line the pastry shells with greaseproof paper and fill with dried beans or rice to weigh down the pastry. Bake in the preheated oven for about 10 minutes, then remove the paper and beans.

Heat the oil in a skillet, add the shallots and fennel, and fry gently for 5 minutes. Sprinkle with the sugar and cook for a further 10 minutes, stirring occasionally until lightly caramelized. Reserve until cooled.

Beat together the egg and cream and season to taste with salt and pepper. Divide the shallot mixture between the pastry shells. Pour over the egg mixture and sprinkle with the cheese and cinnamon. Bake for 20 minutes, until golden and set. Serve with the lettuce leaves.

Try this: FOR AN ALTERNATIVE: 244   FOR KIDS: 242

Black Bean Chili with Avocado Salsa

SERVES 4

1½ cups black beans
   and black-eye beans,
   soaked overnight
2 tbsp olive oil
1 large onion, peeled
   and finely chopped
1 red bell pepper, deseeded
   and diced
2 garlic cloves, peeled
   and finely chopped
1 red chile pepper, deseeded
   and finely chopped

2 tsp chile powder
1 tsp ground cumin
2 tsp ground coriander
14-oz can chopped tomatoes
2 cups vegetable stock
1 small ripe avocado, diced
½ small red onion, peeled
   and finely chopped
2 tbsp freshly
   chopped cilantro
juice of 1 lime
1 small tomato, peeled,

   deseeded, and diced
salt and freshly ground
   black pepper
1 oz dark chocolate

To garnish:
crème fraîche or sour cream
lime slices
sprigs of cilantro

Drain the beans and place in a large saucepan with at least twice their volume of fresh water. Bring slowly to a boil, skimming off any froth that rises to the surface. Boil rapidly for 10 minutes, then reduce the heat and simmer for about 45 minutes, adding more water if necessary. Drain and reserve.

Heat the oil in a large saucepan and add the onion and pepper. Cook for 3–4 minutes until softened. Add the garlic and chile pepper. Cook for 5 minutes, or until the onion and pepper have softened. Add the chile powder, cumin, and coriander, and cook for 30 seconds. Add the beans along with the tomatoes and stock. Bring to a boil and simmer uncovered for 40–45 minutes, until the beans and vegetables are tender and the sauce has reduced.

Mix together the avocado, onion, cilantro, lime juice, and tomato. Season with salt and pepper and set aside. Remove the chili from the heat. Break the chocolate into pieces and sprinkle it over the chili. Let stand for 2 minutes. Stir well. Garnish with sour cream, lime, and cilantro. Serve with the avocado salsa.

Try this: FOR AN ALTERNATIVE: 362 FOR KIDS: 342

Carrot & Parsnip Terrine

SERVES 8-10

6–8 carrots (about 1¼ lb),
   peeled and chopped
4 medium parsnips (about
   1 lb), peeled and chopped
6 tbsp crème fraîche or
   sour cream
8 cups spinach (about 1 lb),
   thoroughly rinsed

1 tbsp brown sugar
1 tbsp freshly
   chopped parsley
½ tsp freshly
   grated nutmeg
salt and freshly ground
   black pepper
6 medium eggs

sprigs of fresh basil,
   to garnish

For the tomato coulis:
4 medium ripe tomatoes,
   deseeded and chopped
1 medium onion, peeled and
   finely chopped

Preheat the oven to 400˚F. Oil and line a 2-lb loaf pan with nonstick baking paper. Cook the carrots and parsnips in boiling salted water for 10–15 minutes, or until tender. Drain and puree separately. Add 2 tablespoons of crème fraîche to both the carrots and the parsnips. Steam the spinach for 5–10 minutes, or until tender. Drain and squeeze out as much liquid as possible, then stir in the remaining crème fraîche.

Add the brown sugar to the carrot puree, the parsley to the parsnip mixture, and the nutmeg to the spinach. Season all to taste with salt and pepper. Beat 2 eggs, add to the spinach, and turn in to the prepared pan. Add another 2 beaten eggs to the carrot mixture and layer carefully on top of the spinach. Beat the remaining eggs into the parsnip puree and layer on top of the terrine. Place the pan in a baking dish and pour in enough hot water to come halfway up the sides of the pan. Bake in the preheated oven for 1 hour, until a skewer inserted into the center comes out clean. Let the terrine cool for at least 30 minutes. Run a sharp knife around the edges. Turn out on to a dish and reserve.

Make the tomato coulis by simmering the tomatoes and onions together for 5–10 minutes, until slightly thickened. Season to taste. Blend well in a blender or food processor and serve as an accompaniment to the terrine. Garnish with sprigs of basil and serve.

Boston–style Baked Beans

SERVES 8

2 cups mixed dried beans,
  such as haricot, flageolet,
  cannellini, pinto beans, or
  chickpeas
1 large onion, peeled and
  finely chopped
½ cup molasses
2 tbsp Dijon mustard

2 tbsp light brown sugar
1 cup all-purpose flour
1 cup fine cornmeal
2 tbsp superfine sugar
2½ tsp baking powder
½ tsp salt
2 tbsp freshly
  chopped thyme

2 medium eggs
1 cup milk
2 tbsp melted butter
salt and freshly ground
  black pepper
parsley sprigs, to garnish

Put the dried beans into a bowl and cover with water. Leave to soak overnight.

Next day, preheat the oven to 250˚F. Drain, rinse, and place the beans in a large saucepan.
Cover with water. Bring to a boil. Boil steadily for 10 minutes then drain the beans and set
aside. Mix together the onion, molasses, mustard, and sugar in a large mixing bowl. Add the
drained beans and 1¼ cups of fresh water. Transfer to an ovenproof dish, cover, and cook in
the preheated oven for 4 hours, stirring once every hour and adding more water if necessary.

When the beans are cooked, remove from the oven and keep warm. Increase the oven
temperature to 400˚F. Mix together the flour, cornmeal, superfine sugar, baking powder,
salt, and most of the thyme, reserving about one–third for garnish. In a separate bowl,
beat the eggs then stir in the milk and butter. Pour the wet ingredients onto the dry ones
and stir just enough to combine.

Pour into a buttered 7-inch square cake pan. Sprinkle over the remaining thyme. Bake for
30 minutes, until golden and risen or until a toothpick inserted into the center comes out
clean. Cut into squares, then reheat the beans. Season to taste with salt and pepper and
serve immediately, garnished with parsley sprigs.

Try this: FOR AN ALTERNATIVE: 358   FOR KIDS: 376

Chargrilled Vegetable
& Goats' Cheese Pizza

SERVES 4

1 medium baking potato
1 tbsp olive oil
2 cups all-purpose flour
½ tsp salt
1 tsp dried yeast

For the topping:
1 medium eggplant,
  thinly sliced
2 small zucchini, trimmed

and sliced lengthways
1 yellow bell pepper,
  quartered and deseeded
1 red onion, peeled and
  sliced into thin wedges
5 tbsp olive oil
4 cooked new potatoes,
  halved
14-oz can chopped
  tomatoes, drained

2 tsp freshly
  chopped oregano
1 cup mozzarella cheese,
  cut into
  small cubes
1 cup goats' cheese,
  crumbled

Preheat the oven to 425°F 15 minutes before baking. Put a baking sheet in the oven to heat up. Cook the potato in lightly salted boiling water until tender. Peel and mash with the olive oil until smooth.

Sift the flour and salt into a bowl. Stir in the yeast. Add the mashed potato and ⅔ cup of warm water and mix to a soft dough. Knead for 5–6 minutes, until smooth. Put the dough in a bowl, cover with plastic wrap, and let rise in a warm place for 30 minutes.

To make the topping, arrange the eggplant, zucchini, pepper, and onion, skin-side up, on a broiler rack and brush with 4 tablespoons of the oil. Broil for 4–5 minutes. Turn the vegetables and brush with the remaining oil. Broil for 3–4 minutes. Cool, skin, and slice the pepper. Put all of the vegetables in a bowl, add the halved new potatoes, and toss gently together. Set aside.

Briefly reknead the dough, then roll out to a 12–14 inch round, according to your preferred thickness. Mix the tomatoes and oregano together and spread over the pizza base. Scatter over the mozzarella cheese and arrange the vegetables and goats' cheese on top. Put the pizza on the preheated baking sheet and bake for 8–10 minutes. Serve.

Try this: FOR AN ALTERNATIVE: 250   FOR KIDS: 344

Rice–filled Peppers

SERVES 4

8 ripe tomatoes
2 tbsp olive oil
1 onion, peeled
   and chopped
1 garlic clove, peeled and
   crushed
½ tsp dark brown sugar

1 cup cooked
   long-grain rice
5½ tbsp pine nuts, toasted
1 tbsp freshly
   chopped oregano
salt and freshly ground
   black pepper

2 large red bell peppers
2 large yellow bell peppers

To serve:
mixed salad
crusty bread

Preheat the oven to 400°F. Put the tomatoes in a small bowl and pour over boiling water to cover. Let stand for 1 minute, then drain. Plunge the tomatoes into cold water to cool, then peel off the skins. Quarter, remove the seeds, and chop.

Heat the olive oil in a skillet and cook the onion gently for 10 minutes, until softened. Add the garlic, chopped tomatoes, and sugar. Gently cook the tomato mixture for 10 minutes, until thickened. Remove from the heat and stir the rice, pine nuts, and oregano into the sauce. Season to taste with salt and pepper.

Halve the peppers lengthways, cutting through and leaving the stem on. Remove the seeds and cores, then put the peppers in a lightly oiled roasting pan, cut-side down, and cook in the preheated oven for about 10 minutes.

Turn the peppers so they are cut-side up. Spoon in the filling, then cover with foil. Return to the oven for 15 minutes, or until the peppers are tender, removing the foil for the last 5 minutes to allow the tops to brown a little.

Serve one red pepper half and one yellow pepper half per person with a mixed salad and plenty of warm crusty bread.

Try this: FOR AN ALTERNATIVE: 270   FOR KIDS: 78

Cabbage Timbale

SERVES 4-6

1 small savoy cabbage,
  (about 12 oz)
salt and freshly ground
  black pepper
2 tbsp olive oil
1 leek, trimmed
  and chopped
1 garlic clove, peeled

and crushed
2½ cups long-grain rice
7-oz can chopped tomatoes
1¼ cups vegetable stock
14-oz can flageolet or navy
  beans, drained and rinsed
¾ cup Cheddar
  cheese, grated

1 tbsp freshly
  chopped oregano

To garnish:
plain yogurt, seasoned
  with paprika
tomato wedges

Preheat the oven to 350°F 10 minutes before required. Remove six of the outer leaves of the cabbage. Cut off the thickest part of the stalk and blanch the leaves in lightly salted boiling water for 2 minutes. Lift out with a slotted spoon and briefly rinse under cold water and reserve. Remove the stalks from the rest of the cabbage leaves. Shred the leaves and blanch in the boiling water for 1 minute. Drain, rinse under cold water, and pat dry on a paper towel.

Heat the oil in a skillet and cook the leek and garlic for 5 minutes. Stir in the rice, chopped tomatoes with their juice, and stock. Bring to a boil, cover, and simmer for 15 minutes. Remove the lid and simmer for a further 4–5 minutes, stirring frequently, until the liquid is absorbed and the rice is tender. Stir in the flageolet beans, cheese, and oregano. Season to taste with salt and pepper.

Line an oiled 1-quart casserole dish with some of the large cabbage leaves, overlapping them slightly. Fill the basin with alternate layers of rice mixture and shredded leaves, pressing down well. Cover the top with the remaining leaves. Cover with oiled foil and bake in the preheated oven for 30 minutes. Let stand for 10 minutes. Turn out, cut into wedges, and serve with yogurt sprinkled with paprika and tomato wedges.

Try this: FOR AN ALTERNATIVE: 336   FOR KIDS: 322

Garlic Wild Mushroom Galettes

SERVES 6

quick flaky pastry (see
  page 242), chilled
1 onion, peeled
1 red chile pepper, deseeded
2 garlic cloves, peeled
4 cups mixed mushrooms,

such as oyster, chestnuts,
  morels, and chanterelles
2 tbsp butter
2 tbsp freshly
  chopped parsley
1 cup mozzarella

cheese, sliced

To serve:
cherry tomatoes
mixed green lettuce leaves

Preheat the oven to 425°F. On a lightly floured surface, roll out the chilled pastry thinly. Cut out six 6-inch circles and place on a lightly oiled baking sheet.

Thinly slice the onion, then divide into rings and reserve. Thinly slice the chile pepper and slice the garlic into wafer-thin slivers. Add to the onions and reserve. Clean the mushrooms. Halve or quarter any large mushrooms and keep the small ones whole.

Heat the butter in a skillet and fry the onion, chile pepper, and garlic gently for 3 minutes. Add the mushrooms and cook for another 5 minutes, or until they begin to soften. Stir the parsley into the mushroom mixture and drain off any excess liquid.

Pile the mushroom mixture onto the pastry circles within ¼ inch of the edge. Arrange the sliced mozzarella cheese on top.

Bake in the preheated oven for 12–15 minutes, or until golden brown, and serve with the tomatoes and salad.

Try this: FOR AN ALTERNATIVE: 376   FOR KIDS: 284

Sweet Corn Cakes

SERVES 6–8

2¼ cups all-purpose flour
3 tbsp Thai red curry paste
2 tbsp light soy sauce
2 tsp sugar
2 kaffir lime leaves , finely
   shredded (optional)
12 fine green beans,
   trimmed, finely chopped,
   and blanched

12-oz can corn kernels,
   drained
salt and freshly ground
   black pepper
2 medium eggs
1 cup fresh white
   bread crumbs
vegetable oil for deep-frying

For the dipping sauce:
2 tbsp hoisin sauce
1 tbsp light brown sugar
1 tbsp sesame oil

To serve:
halved cucumber slices
green onions, sliced
   diagonally

Place the flour in a bowl, make a well in the center, then add the curry paste, soy sauce, and the sugar, along with the shredded kaffir lime leaves (if using), green beans, and corn kernels. Season to taste with salt and pepper, then beat one egg and add to the mixture. Stir in with a fork, adding 1–2 tablespoons of cold water to form a stiff dough. Knead lightly on a floured surface and form into a ball.

Divide the mixture into 16 pieces and shape into small balls, then flatten to form cakes about ½ inch thick and 3 inches in diameter. Beat the remaining egg and pour into a shallow dish. Dip the cakes first in the beaten egg, then in the bread crumbs until lightly coated. Heat the oil in either a wok or deep-fat fryer to 350°F and deep-fry the cakes for 2–3 minutes, or until golden brown. Using a slatted spoon, remove and drain on a paper towel.

Meanwhile, blend the hoisin sauce, sugar, 1 tablespoon of water, and the sesame oil together until smooth and pour into a small bowl. Serve immediately with the sweet corn cakes, cucumber, and green onions.

Try this: FOR AN ALTERNATIVE: 62   FOR KIDS: 144

Fusilli Pasta with Spicy Tomato Salsa

SERVES 4

6 large ripe tomatoes
2 tbsp lemon juice
2 tbsp lime juice
grated rind of 1 lime
2 shallots, peeled and

finely chopped
2 garlic cloves, peeled
and finely chopped
1–2 red chile peppers
1–2 green chile peppers

1 lb fresh fusilli pasta
4 tbsp crème fraîche or
sour cream
2 tbsp freshly chopped basil,
sprig of oregano, to garnish

Place the tomatoes in a bowl and cover with boiling water. Let stand until the skins start to peel away. Remove the skins from the tomatoes, divide each tomato into four, and remove all the seeds. Chop the flesh into small cubes and put in a small pan. Add the lemon and lime juice and the grated lime rind; stir well.

Add the chopped shallots and garlic. Remove the seeds carefully from the chile peppers, chop finely, and add to the pan. Bring to a boil and simmer gently for 5–10 minutes, until the salsa has thickened slightly. Reserve the salsa to allow the flavors to develop while the pasta is cooking.

Bring a large saucepan of water to a boil and add the pasta. Simmer gently for 3–4 minutes, or until the pasta is just tender.

Drain the pasta and rinse in boiling water. Top with a large spoonful of salsa and a small spoonful of crème fraîche. Garnish with the chopped basil and oregano and serve immediately.

Try this: FOR AN ALTERNATIVE: 332   FOR KIDS: 290

Mushroom Stew

SERVES 4

4 dried porcini mushrooms
2 lb assorted fresh
   mushrooms, cleaned
2 tbsp virgin olive oil
1 onion, peeled and
   finely chopped
2 garlic cloves, peeled and
   finely chopped

1 tbsp fresh thyme leaves
pinch of ground cloves
salt and freshly ground
   black pepper
5–6 medium tomatoes
   (about 1½ lb), peeled,
   deseeded, and chopped
1⅓ cups instant polenta

2½ cups vegetable stock
3 tbsp freshly chopped
   mixed herbs
sprigs of parsley, to garnish

Soak the porcini mushrooms in a small bowl of hot water for 20 minutes. Drain, reserving both the mushrooms and their soaking liquor. Cut the fresh mushrooms in half and reserve.

In a saucepan, heat the oil and add the onion. Cook gently for 5–7 minutes, until softened. Add the garlic, thyme, and cloves and continue cooking for 2 minutes.

Add all the mushrooms and cook for 8–10 minutes, until the mushrooms have softened, stirring often. Season to taste with salt and pepper, and add the tomatoes and the reserved soaking liquid.

Simmer, partly covered, over a low heat for about 20 minutes, until thickened. Adjust the seasoning to taste.

Meanwhile, cook the polenta according to the package instructions, using the vegetable stock. Stir in the herbs and divide between four dishes. Ladle the mushrooms over the polenta, garnish with the parsley, and serve immediately.

Creamy Lentils

SERVES 4

1¼ cups puy or other lentils
1 tbsp olive oil
1 garlic clove, peeled and
    finely chopped
zest and juice of 1 lemon
1 tsp whole-grain mustard
1 tbsp freshly

chopped tarragon
3 tbsp crème fraîche or
    sour cream
salt and freshly ground
    black pepper
2 small tomatoes, deseeded
    and chopped

10 large, pitted black olives
1 tbsp freshly
    chopped parsley

To garnish:
sprigs of fresh tarragon
lemon wedges

Put the lentils in a saucepan with plenty of cold water and bring to a boil. Boil rapidly for 10 minutes, reduce the heat, and simmer gently for a further 20 minutes, until just tender. Drain well.

Meanwhile, prepare the dressing. Heat the oil in a skillet over a medium heat. Add the garlic and cook for about a minute, until it just begins to brown. Add the lemon zest and juice.

Add the mustard and cook for a further 30 seconds. Add the tarragon and crème fraîche, and season to taste with salt and pepper.

Simmer and add the drained lentils, tomatoes, and olives. Transfer to a serving dish and sprinkle the chopped parsley on top. Garnish the lentils with the tarragon sprigs and the lemon wedges and serve immediately.

Try this: FOR AN ALTERNATIVE: 342   FOR KIDS: 362

Sweet Potato Chips with Mango Salsa

SERVES 6

For the salsa:
1 large, ripe mango, peeled, stoned, and cut into small cubes
8 cherry tomatoes, quartered
½ cucumber, peeled if preferred and finely diced

1 red onion, peeled and finely chopped
pinch of sugar
1 red chile pepper, deseeded and finely chopped
2 tbsp rice vinegar
2 tbsp olive oil
grated rind and

juice of 1 lime
2 tbsp freshly chopped mint

2 large sweet potatoes (about 1 lb), peeled and thinly sliced
vegetable oil, for deep-frying
sea salt

To make the salsa, mix the mango with the tomatoes, cucumber, and onion. Add the sugar, chile pepper, vinegar, oil, and the lime rind and juice. Mix together thoroughly, cover, and let stand for 45–50 minutes.

Soak the potatoes in cold water for 40 minutes to remove as much of the excess starch as possible. Drain and dry thoroughly in a clean kitchen towel or paper towel.

Heat the oil to 375°F in a deep fryer. When at the correct temperature, place half the potatoes in the frying basket, then carefully lower the potatoes into the hot oil and cook for 4–5 minutes, or until they are golden brown, shaking the basket every minute so that they do not stick together.

Drain the potato chips on a paper towel, sprinkle with sea salt, and place under a preheated moderate broiler for a few seconds to dry out. Repeat with the remaining potatoes. Stir the mint into the salsa and serve with the potato chips.

Try this: FOR AN ALTERNATIVE: 156   FOR KIDS: 180

Index

Index